It's another Quality Book from CGP

This book is for 11-14 year olds.

First we stick in all the really important stuff you need to write good English.

Then we have a real good stab at trying to make it funny — so you'll actually use it.

Simple as that.

What CGP is all about

Our sole aim here at CGP is to produce the highest quality books — carefully written, immaculately presented, and dangerously close to being funny.

Then we work our socks off to get them out to you — at the cheapest possible prices.

Contents

Section One — Nouns and Pronouns

Section Two — Punctuation

Section Three — Writing Proper Sentences

Section Four — Paragraphs

Section Five — Handwriting and Spelling

Section Six — Writing

Section Seven — Confusing Words

Section Eight — Reading

Published by Coordination Group Publications Ltd.

Contributors:
Taissa Csáky
Gemma Hallam
Dominic Hall
Simon Little
Glenn Rogers
Laura Schibrowski
Katherine Stewart
Claire Thompson
Tim Wakeling
James Paul Wallis
Andrew Wright

And:
Simon Cook
Chris Dennett
Kate Stevens

ISBN: 978 1 84146 145 8

Groovy website: www.cgpbooks.co.uk
Jolly bits of clipart from CorelDRAW®
Printed by Elanders Hindson Ltd, Newcastle upon Tyne.

Nouns

Any word that means a thing (like a person, an animal, a place, or even a turnip) is called a noun.

Nouns are words for Things

In other words, nouns are just the names of things.
Here are a few everyday ones:

woman, tree, hedgehog, balloon

Grrr!
Sally

It could also be the name of something like a person, a place, a day or a month. Watch out though — these always have a capital letter...

Sally, Wales, Tuesday, November

Those are names of types of things or a single thing, but words for groups of things are also nouns:

herd, flock, team, bundle

Not All Nouns are things you can Touch

Be careful though — some nouns are names of those weird things that you can't see, touch or hear:

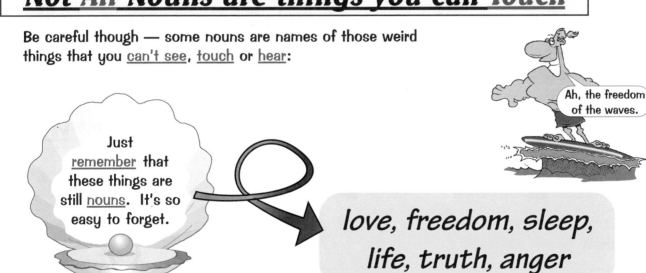

Ah, the freedom of the waves.

Just remember that these things are still nouns. It's so easy to forget.

love, freedom, sleep, life, truth, anger

Noun — not the middle of the day...

It'll be much easier later on if you know what a noun is. So learn the four kinds now:
1) a type of thing, 2) a single thing, 3) a group of things, 4) a thing you can't touch (an idea).

Plurals

Plural means 'more than one'. Most words add an 's' to show that there's more than one. Unluckily, not all words are that easy — you have to learn all the weird ones too.

Most words add '-s' to make the plural

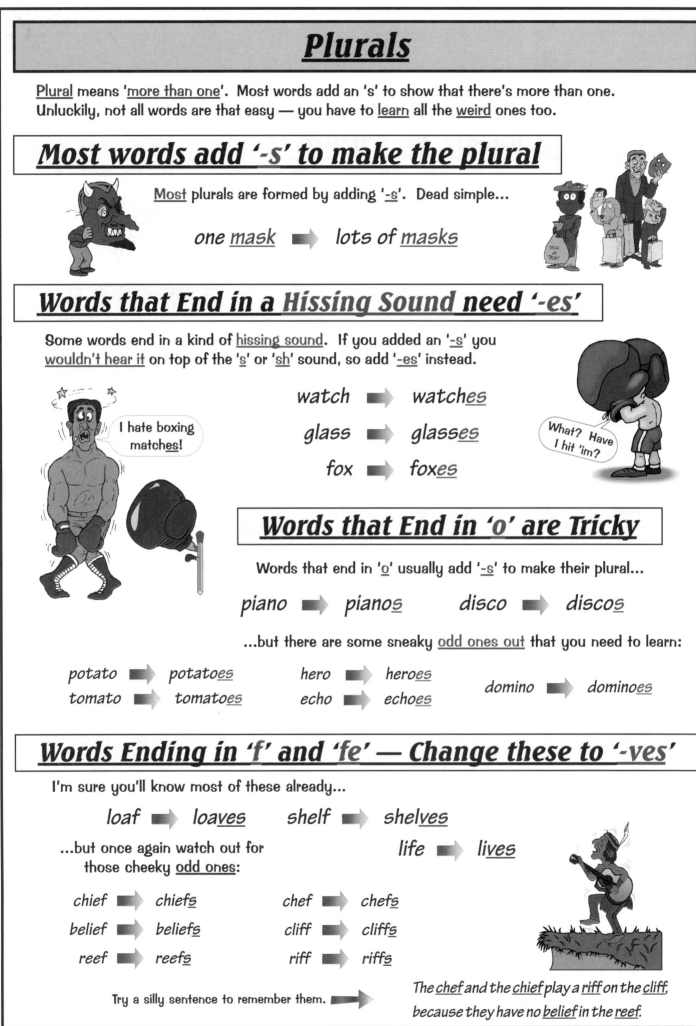

Most plurals are formed by adding '-s'. Dead simple...

one mask → lots of masks

Words that End in a Hissing Sound need '-es'

Some words end in a kind of hissing sound. If you added an '-s' you wouldn't hear it on top of the 's' or 'sh' sound, so add '-es' instead.

What? Have I hit 'im?

I hate boxing matches!

watch → watches

glass → glasses

fox → foxes

Words that End in 'o' are Tricky

Words that end in 'o' usually add '-s' to make their plural...

piano → pianos   disco → discos

...but there are some sneaky odd ones out that you need to learn:

potato → potatoes   hero → heroes   domino → dominoes

tomato → tomatoes   echo → echoes

Words Ending in 'f' and 'fe' — Change these to '-ves'

I'm sure you'll know most of these already...

loaf → loaves   shelf → shelves   life → lives

...but once again watch out for those cheeky odd ones:

chief → chiefs   chef → chefs

belief → beliefs   cliff → cliffs

reef → reefs   riff → riffs

Try a silly sentence to remember them. → *The chef and the chief play a riff on the cliff, because they have no belief in the reef.*

Plurals

Words that End in 'y'

This needs a bit of thought. Some of these words take '-s' to make the plural. Others change the 'y' to 'ies'. You just have to look at the letter before the 'y':

If the letter before the 'y' is a vowel, then just add '-s' for the plural. If the letter before the 'y' is a consonant, the 'y' becomes '-ies' for the plural.

A vowel is one of these: a e i o u. Anything else is a consonant.

Confused? Check out these examples:

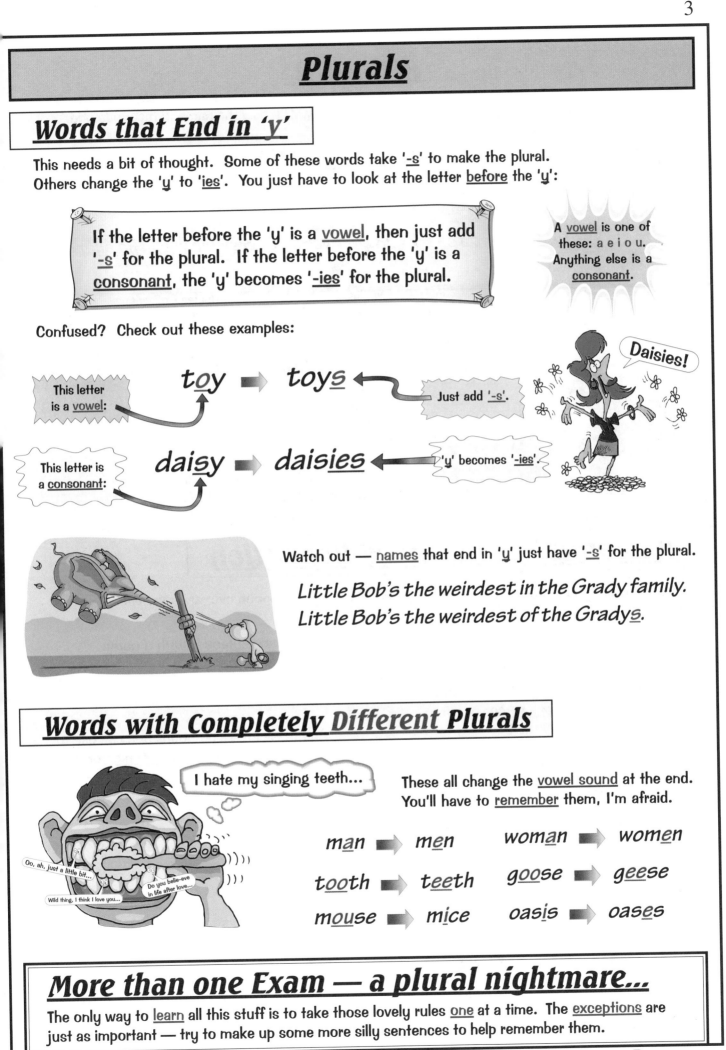

Watch out — names that end in 'y' just have '-s' for the plural.

Little Bob's the weirdest in the Grady family.
Little Bob's the weirdest of the Gradys.

Words with Completely Different Plurals

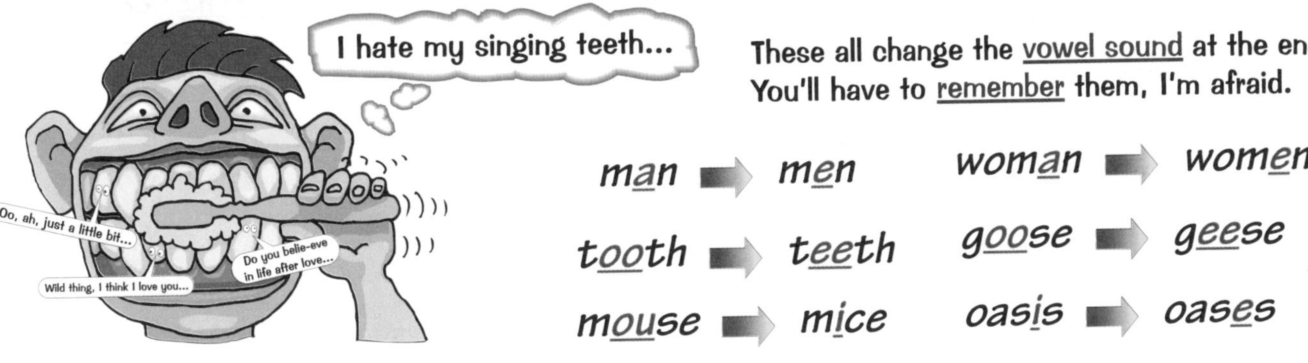

I hate my singing teeth...
Oo, ah, just a little bit...
Do you belie-eve in life after love...
Wild thing, I think I love you...

These all change the vowel sound at the end. You'll have to remember them, I'm afraid.

man →	men	woman →	women
tooth →	teeth	goose →	geese
mouse →	mice	oasis →	oases

More than one Exam — a plural nightmare...

The only way to learn all this stuff is to take those lovely rules one at a time. The exceptions are just as important — try to make up some more silly sentences to help remember them.

Pronouns

Pronouns are little everyday words that you already know. It's only the name that sounds odd.

Pronouns go instead of Nouns

The sentence below looks a bit odd. You don't need to write 'Bob' or 'shark' twice.

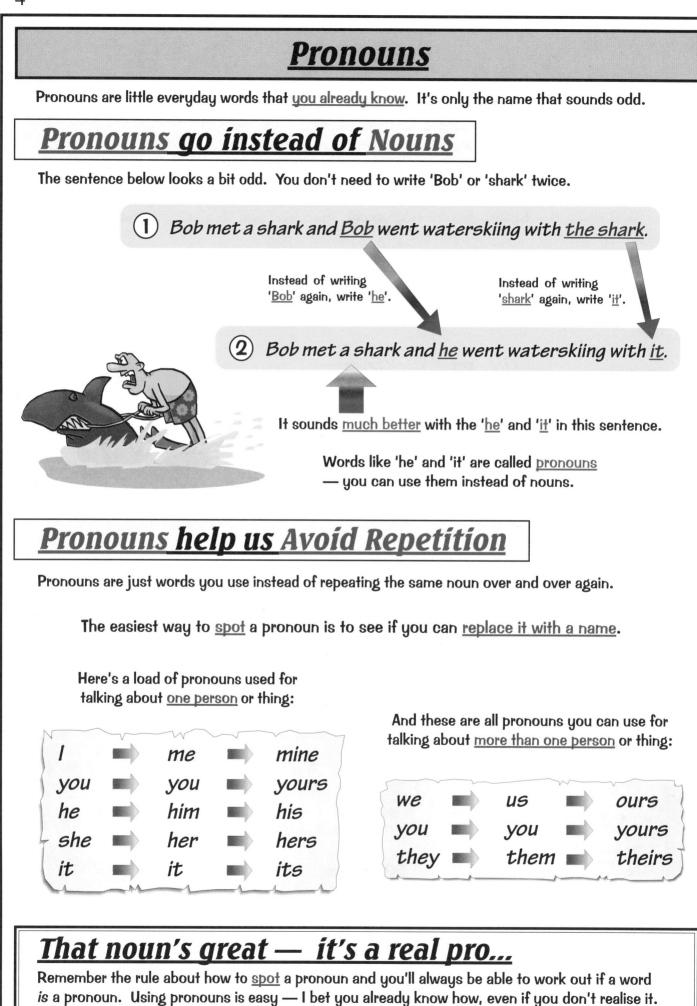

① *Bob met a shark and Bob went waterskiing with the shark.*

Instead of writing 'Bob' again, write 'he'.

Instead of writing 'shark' again, write 'it'.

② *Bob met a shark and he went waterskiing with it.*

It sounds much better with the 'he' and 'it' in this sentence.

Words like 'he' and 'it' are called pronouns — you can use them instead of nouns.

Pronouns help us Avoid Repetition

Pronouns are just words you use instead of repeating the same noun over and over again.

The easiest way to spot a pronoun is to see if you can replace it with a name.

Here's a load of pronouns used for talking about one person or thing:

I → me → mine
you → you → yours
he → him → his
she → her → hers
it → it → its

And these are all pronouns you can use for talking about more than one person or thing:

we → us → ours
you → you → yours
they → them → theirs

That noun's great — it's a real pro...

Remember the rule about how to spot a pronoun and you'll always be able to work out if a word *is* a pronoun. Using pronouns is easy — I bet you already know how, even if you don't realise it. The thing to remember is to use them instead of repeating the same noun over and over again.

Beginning & Ending a Sentence

You need a capital letter to start a sentence, and a full stop to end it. Sounds pretty simple, so there ought to be no excuse for forgetting them.

Always Start a Sentence with a Capital Letter

Every single sentence starts with a capital letter. Don't you ever forget them.

Roland had always dreamed of being the first mouse to land on the moon. He lit the fuse and with a mighty roar, his home-made wax rocket blasted into space.

A full stop finishes each sentence.

It's made of cheese, you know.
Yeah and pigs can...
Good day old chaps!

A capital letter starts each sentence.

Biggleswoth followed him in his toilet-paper aeroplane. The trip ended in disaster when they were both sucked up by a giant black mole.

Haha!

In some sentences you replace the full stop with something else.

Question Marks go at the End of Questions

Any sentence asking a question must end with a question mark instead of a full stop.

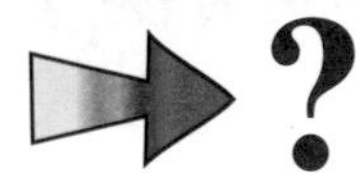

Put a question mark instead of a full stop.

Would you like me to eat you?

Charlie asked the goldfish if it would like to be eaten.

This sentence tells you about a question, but it doesn't ask one. So you don't need a question mark.

There's no question mark here.

Exclamation Marks show strong feelings!

This groovy symbol is an exclamation mark. You'll need one at the end of a sentence which shows a strong feeling.

Go away!

Stop it!

Leave him alone!

It was brilliant!

You can use an exclamation mark:

1) if the sentence is a command.
2) for someone shouting.
3) to show surprise or anger.

Remember — exclamation marks and question marks replace the full stop. Don't put a full stop in as well.

Capital Letters — L is for London...

This is monstrously important. Capital letters and full stops are obvious, but you have to remember to put them in all the time. Check your work to make sure they're all there.

Showing Who Owns What

Apostrophes are the little comma-shaped squiggles used to show when something belongs to somebody. Learn all about them or you'll make dead nasty mistakes.

Adding 's' to show Who Owns What

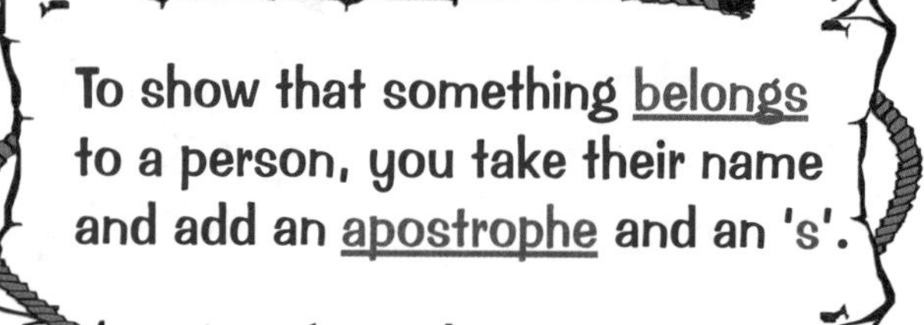

To show that something belongs to a person, you take their name and add an apostrophe and an 's'.

Kylie's hair is bright green.

Sophie's mice have grown very fat.

But if it Already Ends in 's'...

If the name already ends with an 's', add an apostrophe and another 's'. You can just add an apostrophe, but apostrophe and 's' is better.

James's bike has been flattened.

Magnus' dog has got fleas.

Watch out, though. Some names are only written one way. All you can do is learn them, I'm afraid.

Jesus' disciples *St James's Park*

For Groups of People...

If it's a word for a group of people or a group of things which ends in 's', all you do is stick an apostrophe on the end.

I washed the neighbours' windows with orangeade.

I guess they needed a wash...

Words like men, women and mice are easy. Just add an apostrophe and an 's'.

I put the men's shoes in the toilet and the women's shoes in the pond.

It's all mine — OWN-ly joking...

You use apostrophe 's' unless it's a plural that ends in 's'. Unfortunately, there are a few pesky exceptions that need learning. To make life easier, the page is divided up into sections for each one.

Show Missing Letters with an ’

Here's something else that you need apostrophes for. Apostrophes are used to make short forms of words, like we're for 'we are' and she's for 'she is'. Learn how to do it now.

Making Two words into One

I've is the short form of 'I have'. When you write it, you have to put an apostrophe in to show that the 'ha' is missing.

Here are some more that you can shorten into one word. Remember — the apostrophe goes where the letters have been removed.

I am	I'm
I have	I've
we are	we're
do not	don't
who is	who's
does not	doesn't

I would	I'd
I had	I'd
can not	can't
they are	they're

Here are a couple more shortened words that are a bit less obvious:

shall not	shan't
will not	won't

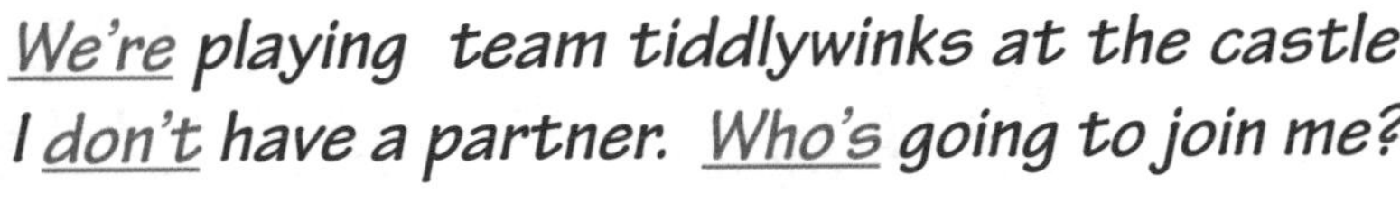

We're playing team tiddlywinks at the castle.
I don't have a partner. Who's going to join me?

We shan't play tonight, we're washing our hare.

I hate being bathed.
Waaaaaaaaa!

Oh, it doesn't matter. I'll go on my own.

Don't use Apostrophes for More Than One

Never use an apostrophe for plurals (when you talk about more than one of something). People often do this, but it's completely wrong.

Granny goes rollerblading with my friend's. 

Granny goes rollerblading with my friends. ✓

I'm hip.
I'm with it.

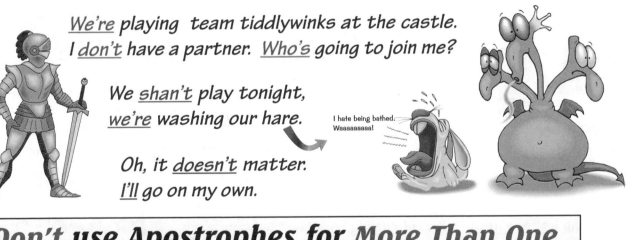

Missing letters? — see your postman...

Don't forget to put in your apostrophe when there are letters missing. It makes your writing make sense. If you miss out the apostrophe you sometimes get a different word — for example he'll = he will, hell = fire and brimstone. Learn this, too: never EVER use 's for a standard plural.

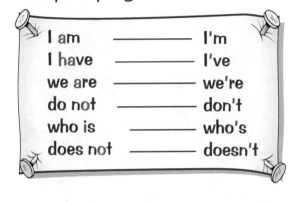

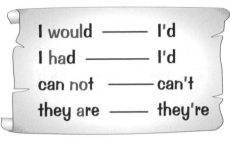

Commas in Lists

Commas are dead important. Make sure you learn how to use them.

Commas Break things up in a List

When you have a list, you need those commas. This example shows you why:

I like roast chicken pizza ice cream and chips. ✗

You don't want the reader to think you're talking about ice cream which is 'roast chicken and pizza' flavoured.

So you put commas to separate each thing in the list. Like this:

I like roast chicken, pizza, ice cream and chips. ✓

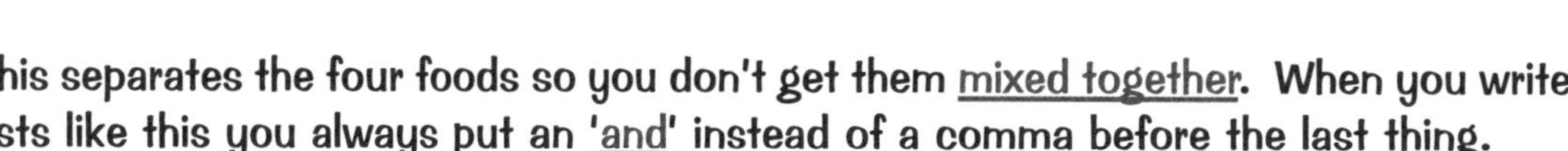

This separates the four foods so you don't get them mixed together. When you write lists like this you always put an 'and' instead of a comma before the last thing.

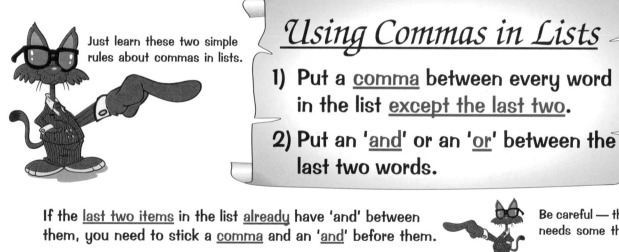

Just learn these two simple rules about commas in lists.

Using Commas in Lists

1) Put a comma between every word in the list except the last two.
2) Put an 'and' or an 'or' between the last two words.

If the last two items in the list already have 'and' between them, you need to stick a comma and an 'and' before them.

Be careful — this bit needs some thought.

We had soup, salad, and steak and chips.

It needs this comma to separate the 'salad' from the 'steak and chips'.

Comma, comma, comma, comma, comma Chameleon...

Using commas in lists really isn't hard. The trouble comes when people get careless and start missing commas out even though they know deep down that they shouldn't. Learn the rules, and every time you write a list, think 'commas'. Don't lose marks on the easy stuff.

Commas in Long Sentences

And there's more, hurrah! You also need commas in long sentences to break them up.

Commas can make the Meaning more Clear

Commas break up long sentences to make them easier to understand. Some sentences have more than one point. You need a comma to keep the different points separate.

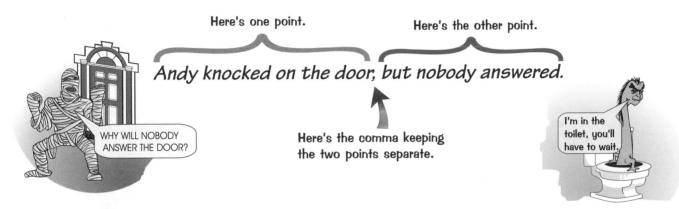

Here's one point. Here's the other point.

Andy knocked on the door, but nobody answered.

Here's the comma keeping the two points separate.

WHY WILL NOBODY ANSWER THE DOOR?

I'm in the toilet, you'll have to wait.

Commas help you put Extra Bits in a sentence

Commas make it easy to add extra bits to a sentence to make it more interesting.

I broke the table in half.

With a loud yell, I broke the table in half.

Extra information to make the sentence more interesting.

You need a comma to separate it from the main part of the sentence.

Katy and Kevin are teaching us martial arts.

Katy and Kevin, the Karate Twins, are teaching us martial arts.

This extra bit is given in the middle of the sentence, so you put commas before and after it.

Words like 'Oh' and 'Well' need a Comma

When you start a sentence with a word like 'Oh' or 'Well', you need a comma to separate it from the rest of the sentence.

Well, you wouldn't believe what happened next.

Oh, it wasn't that bad.

Commas — not full stops with beards...

Grrr — another page about commas. Luckily for you, it's split up into three easy-to-learn sections. Commas in long sentences are a bit grisly, but they are definitely worth learning if you want your work to be easy to read. Just don't forget to use them with words like 'Oh' and 'Well'.

Speech Marks

Don't be scared of speech marks. They do just what the name says — they show when someone's speaking. All you've got to do is use them in all the right places.

Speech Marks show when Someone is Speaking

Every time you write the actual words someone speaks, you need to use speech marks. Speech marks go before and after the words spoken.

We go before the speech.

We go after it.

"Are you sure that this is the footpath?" asked Ted.

Speech marks go at the start of the speech.

And also at the end of the speech, like this.

"This way is very steep," he explained.
"Actually, I think I'm going to fall now."

You need speech marks because these are the actual words that Ted said.

When to Use Speech Marks

Be careful. Sometimes you might write about what someone has said, without actually using their words.

Get rid of it!

Bill said that he wasn't afraid of the spider.

NO SPEECH MARKS

You don't need speech marks here because there's no actual speech in the sentence.

Bill said, "I'm not afraid of the spider."

SPEECH MARKS

This time Bill's words are used in the sentence, so you do need them.

Marks — watch them or you'll lose your speech...

OK, this is the easy bit about speech marks — when to use them. The main thing to remember is that you don't need them if there's no actual speech — like if you're not writing their actual words.

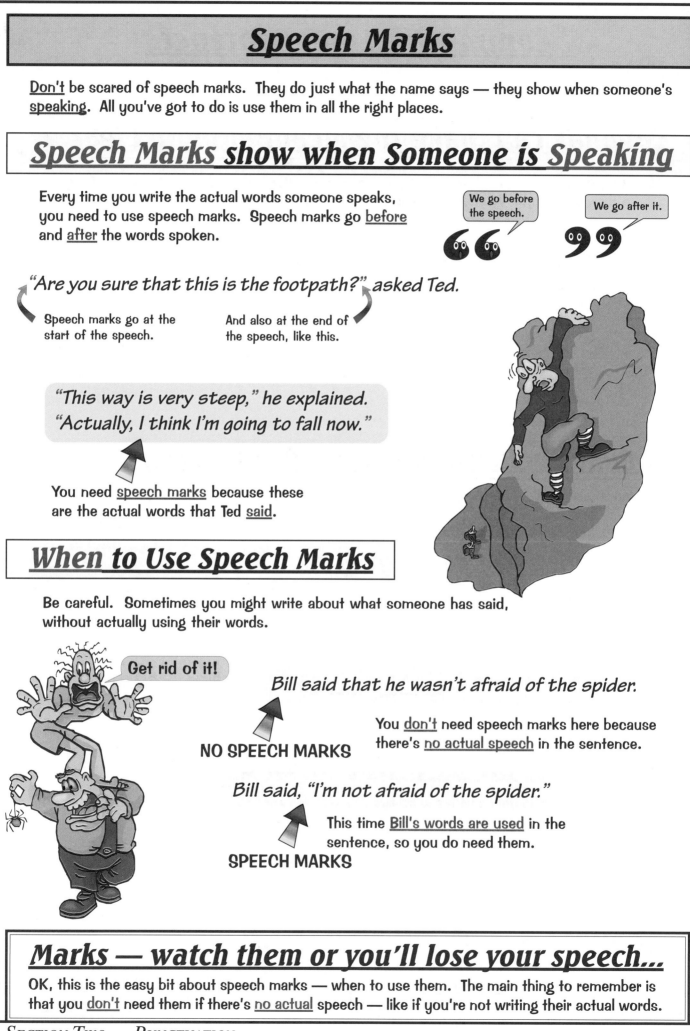

Speech Marks and Punctuation

Here are some cunning little rules about writing speech in speech marks. Some of it's a little bit hard to remember, so get practising till it all sinks in...

Start with a Capital Letter

He added, "You would have loved it."

The spoken bit always starts with a capital letter, even if it isn't at the beginning of the sentence.

Speech Always ends with a Punctuation Mark

It's important that you end the speech properly. It's not hard, but you need to remember the rules:

If the sentence ends when the speech ends, put a full stop before the closing speech mark.

If the sentence continues after the speech, put a comma before the closing speech marks.

If the speech is a command or shows strong feelings, put an exclamation mark there instead.

If the speech is a question, put a question mark there.

Lenny said, "It smells terrible."

The sentence is finished, so you need a full stop.

"I think it's stuck down there," Bob added.

The speech has finished but the sentence hasn't. You need a comma here, not a full stop.

"No way!" yelled Bob.

Bob is shouting, so it needs an exclamation mark.

"How did you get down there?" he asked.

This is a question, so here's a nice question mark.

Speech marks — six out of ten?...

Right, now the harder bit — speech marks and punctuation. There's two main points:
1) Speech always starts with a capital letter. 2) It always ends with a punctuation mark — make sure you know when it should be a full stop, comma, question mark and exclamation mark.

Revision Summary for Sections 1 & 2

I know punctuation can get a bit tedious, but at least it's useful. The trouble is, reading through a section isn't the best way to learn it — the best way is practice. If you really want to improve your punctuation, think about it whenever you write something, and go back over it afterwards to check it's okay. Think about it when you're reading too — look at where writers put in their commas. Before any of that though, have a go at these questions. They're just going over the stuff in this book, but they'll tell you which bits you know and which you don't. All you need to answer them is in the first two sections, so look back if you're stuck...

1) OK, a bit of a tricky one to start you off. Which of these words is *not* a noun: donkey, Henry, loved, radish.
2) This one's not much better. Which of these *isn't* a noun: Saturday, lettuce, bunch, angry.
3) What are the four different types of noun? Give an example for each one.
4) What does that nasty word 'plural' mean?
5) Some words add 'es' instead of 's' to form the plural. How can you tell if you should add 'es'?
6) What are the plurals of 'piano', 'echo', 'tomato' and 'domino'?
7) How do you usually form the plurals of words ending in 'f' or 'fe'?
8) Give six cheeky words with plurals that end in 'fs'.
9) If a word ends in 'y', what's the rule to work out its plural?
10) What are the plurals of 'daisy', 'woman', 'goose' and 'oasis'?
11) Is a pronoun: a) a word you use instead of a noun, or b) a noun that gets paid?
12) Which of these tricksters isn't a pronoun: his, hers, Bob's, mine.
13) What are the other two pronouns that go with 'you'?
14) Should you start a sentence with: a) a capital letter, or b) a goldfish.
15) Name three times when you can end a sentence with an exclamation mark.
16) Put apostrophes in the right places in these sentences:
    a) Jesus disciples spotted Harrys donkey.
    b) The childrens bikes were allowed, but their parents cars werent.
    c) My friends all think I cant write properly because I dont put in any apostrophes.
17) Put commas in the right places in these sentences:
    a) I saw lions giraffes hippos and a huge alien donkey-snatcher.
    b) Kate and Bob the turnip growers can grow me a turnip any day.
    c) I ate a whole elephant though it was just a chocolate one.
    d) "Oh my head's just fallen off" thought Kevin.
18) OK, the last one now. See if you can add the punctuation to these:
    a) I'm in heaven thought Clarissa
    b) Go away shouted Cecil
    c) Whats that got to do with me asked Esmerelda Floggarty
    d) Emma suddenly said Oops there goes my clog

Sentences

OK, it's time to look at how sentences work. Writing proper sentences is the key to getting absolutely everything else in English right — pretty important, I'd say.

A Sentence Makes Sense on its Own

1. Get this straight. Everything you write must be in proper sentences, and every sentence must make sense on its own.

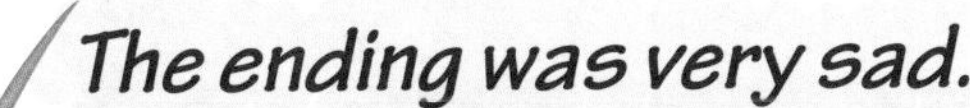

✓ *The ending was very sad.*

This is a proper sentence. You can see what it means.

✗ *The way it ended.*

This isn't a proper sentence. You can't tell what it's trying to say.

2. If you can't understand what it's supposed to be about, it's not a proper sentence.

✗ *They skated upside-down. Starting with Denzel.*

The second sentence doesn't make sense by itself, so it's not a proper sentence.

Either make them into one sentence, or make the second one make sense by itself:

✓ *They skated upside-down, starting with Denzel.*

✓ *They skated upside-down. Denzel went first.*

A Sentence Makes a Clear Point

Today is Tuesday.

I can't see anything.

You smell of turnip toast.

This means that you've got to know what you want to say in the sentence.

Sometimes you have to think a little first, but that's better than writing a lot of rubbish that doesn't really say anything.

Ten years — that's what I call a sentence...

Writing is all about making sense, so you've got to make sure that every single thing you write does just that. Think about what you want to say first to make sure it hits the spot.

Verbs in Sentences

Yup, this is a page of boring grammar. The point of it all is to help you write proper sentences. Learn what a verb is, and make sure you never write a sentence without one.

A Verb is a Doing or Being word

This is a 'doing' word.

The surgeons are ready.

This one's a 'being' word.

Every Sentence needs a Verb

Here's a nice, easy rule to learn. It's very simple:
Every sentence you write must have at least one verb in it.

Henry surfed into a giant cucumber.

These are the verbs. Some verbs are made of two separate words.

Emily is eating a turnip.

If there isn't a verb, then your sentence won't be about anything, and it won't make sense.

He won the Cup in 1992. And also in 1994.

This doesn't have a verb.
It isn't a proper sentence.

Instead it should be, "He won the cup in 1992, and also in 1994".

Sage, rosemary, thyme — No, I said VERBS...

The key to getting your sentence to make sense is to make sure it's got a verb. Look at each sentence on its own, check it's got a verb and check it makes sense.

Tricky Stuff in the Past Tense

You'll need these all the time, so scribble them down and learn them — but watch those spellings.

General Tricky Stuff

You use these all the time, but some are easy to mix up — read it carefully, till you've learnt them.

NOW	THEN (in the past)		
I begin	I began	OR	I have begun
I break	I broke	OR	I have broken
I fly	I flew	OR	I have flown
I hang	I hung	OR	I have hung
I shrink	I shrank	OR	I have shrunk
I stink	I stank	OR	I have stunk

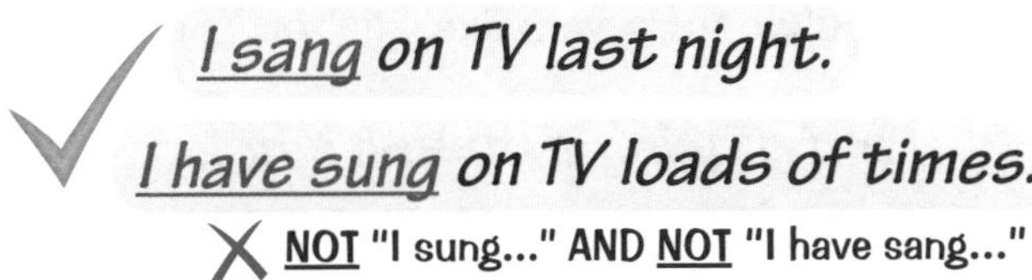

I sang on TV last night.
I have sung on TV loads of times.

NOT "I sung..." AND NOT "I have sang..."

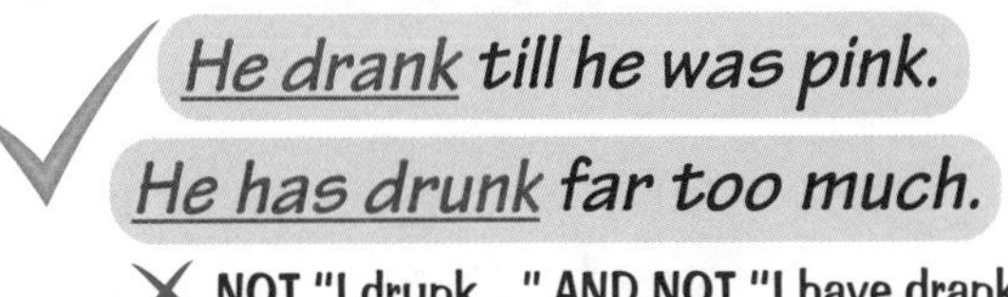

He drank till he was pink.
He has drunk far too much.

NOT "I drunk..." AND NOT "I have drank..."

I watched as they swam to Spain.

I'm not sure if they have swum before.

NOT "they swum..." AND NOT "they have swam..."

Say "He's trodden on it", NOT "He's trod on it"

Sometimes these might sound okay at first if you miss off the '-en' bit. But that's WRONG.

Have you spoken to him?

NOT "Have you spoke to him?"

It is hidden in the mud.

NOT "It is hid in the mud."

We've forgotten the melons.

NOT "We've forgot the melons."

You've trodden on it.

NOT "You've trod on it."

It's all shaken up.

NOT "It's all shook up."
(Whatever Elvis might've said.)

BUT! The odd one out: GOT.
I have got wet.
Only Americans say 'gotten'.

Say "I lay in bed", NOT "I've laid in bed"

SAY THIS: *I lay in bed till 5pm.*

NOT "I laid in bed till 5pm."

('Laid' is only for tables and things like that.)

SAY THIS: *I have lain here all day.*

NOT "I have laid here all day."

Spelling '-ing' Words

The basic problem that people have with these verbs is that they can't spell them properly.

Watch out for Verbs like 'Dig', 'Shop' and 'Slip'

When you've got a verb like 'dig' or 'slip', you need to double the letter before the -ing.

I am digging a massive hole. NOT diging.

Dog Boy keeps slipping on banana skins. NOT sliping.

I hate shopping. NOT shoping.

I'm putting another letter on.

When you add -ing to verbs like this, you've got to double the last letter. → *shopping* *putting*

Most words with short sounds double the last letter.

Short sound: *tap* → *tapping* BUT Long sound: *tape* → *taping*

TAPE TAPE

Be careful — miss out the double letter, and you'll say daft things like "I was taping on the door."

Longer words are tricky. Some double (beginning, preferring...) — but then some don't (offering).

Chop off Silent 'e' Endings Before You Add '-ing'

You've got to chop off the 'e' from 'race'.

The snails are racing each other.

Chop it off!

Always chop off the '-e' before '-ing'. It's a whopper of a mistake if you don't.

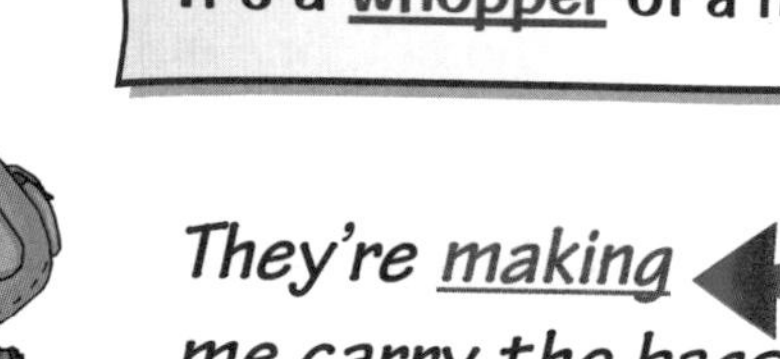

They're making me carry the bags. ← No 'e' here either.

Here you need to chop the 'e' off 'take'.

You're taking us for a ride.

Words like lie, die go like this with a 'y'.  *I'm dying for a squirrel sandwich.*

But it dosn't mak sns if you chop off th 'e's...

Your best bet is just to learn these rules. Remember — verbs with long vowel sounds like 'ee', 'ea', 'oo' always just add -ing. The biggest mistake people make is with those pesky silent 'e's. Learn this — if the 'e' is silent, cut it out before you put the -ing on.

Spelling '-ed' Words

This is where you need to keep your eyes open. It's not the most exciting stuff, but dead essential...

Most Verbs have '-ed' added for the Past...

She stayed away.

He walked two miles.

They laughed.

...But Some Verbs end in '-t' Instead

Some verbs end in '-t'. The best thing to do is learn the common ones.

Crazy Daisy dealt the cards. (deal)

I meant exactly what I said. (mean)

Poddy left at 9am. (leave)

With these ones, you can choose '-ed' OR '-t'.

learn	smell
lean	spell
leap	spill
burn	spoil

We smelled him.

We smelt him.

Watch it — the double 'l' ones only keep one 'l' before the '-t'.

Watch out for verbs with 'ee' in the middle. Lose one 'e' and stick a '-t' on the end.

We crept into the barn. (creep)

I slept badly. (sleep)

Dilly kept scaring the swimmers. (keep)

(sweep) swept (kneel) knelt (weep) wept

Some Verbs like 'stop' and 'sob' add a letter

It's just like when you're adding -ing (see the top of the last page).

He sobbed like a baby.

After two hours, he stopped.

But I thought 'verbs' ended in 's'...

Yes, I know these are boring spellings, but I'm afraid you do need to know them. I expect you know most of them anyway — but do make a note of those you don't know, and make sure you learn them.

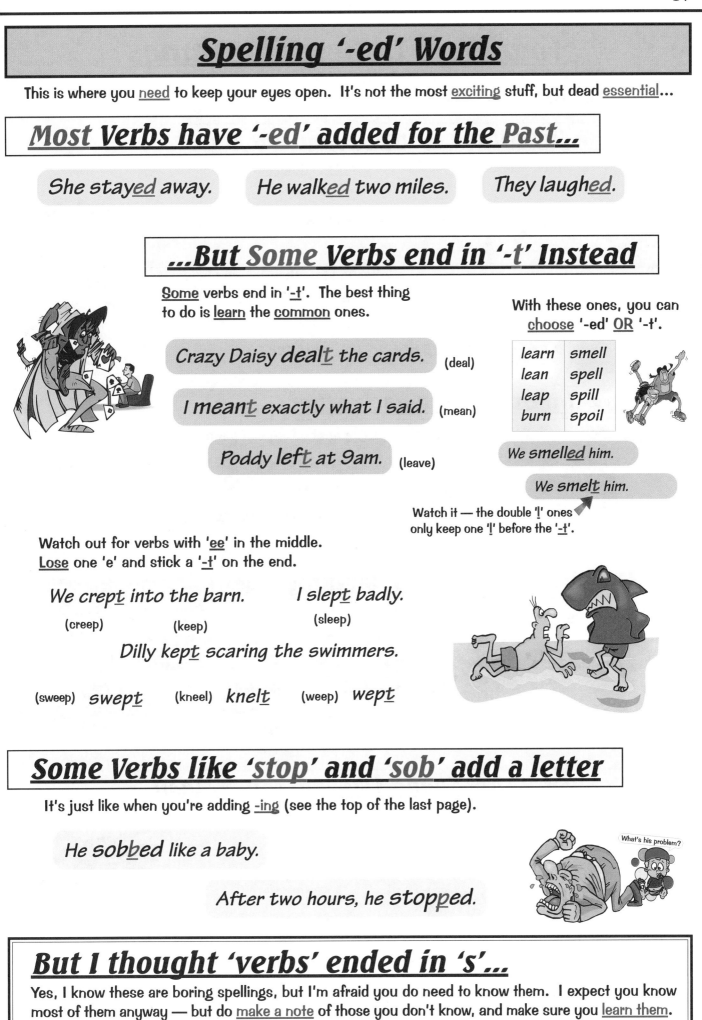

Four Ways to Describe Things

Describing things well is a very useful trick. Here's how it's done...

1) Use Describing Words to tell you More

Describing words tell you more about the people or things in the sentence and give a better picture of what's going on.

There are tall, thin, blue men in my house.

These describe the men.

Describing words can bring a story or a letter to life. They tell you how the characters were feeling, and what the mood of a scene was like.

The strange men looked frightening.
Nervous, I spread out my bright feathers.

2) Say things are Like each other

You can say one thing is like another — comparing them.

Max's shadow was huge and menacing, like Frankenstein's monster.

This is called a simile.

3) Say something Is Something else

You can say one thing is another — when you mean it's like the other thing.

His dad is a real ogre.

This is called a metaphor.

This doesn't mean his dad is a man-eating giant. It means he is strict and nasty.

4) Use words that Sound Like what they Mean

Some words sound a bit like what they're talking about:

Crunch! The car smashed as Max drove over it.

This is called onomatopoeia.

Get a better picture — buy a new camera...

Writing interesting sentences is a big part of doing well at English. It's actually not as hard as it seems. Just try to use words that give you a good clear picture of what you're talking about.

More and Most

Sometimes you'll need to write sentences about who or what is the best. Sounds easy enough, but there are a few little tricks to watch out for. Make sure you learn this page carefully.

When it's More — only add -er to Short Words

You can add -er to short describing words, but you have to use 'more... than' for longer words.

Bob is smarter than Pam.

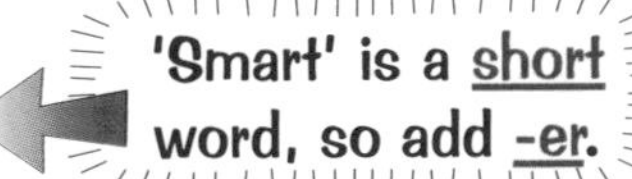

Well, I'm short. Why can't they add er to me?
er

Ellie is more beautiful than Billie.

You don't write 'beautifuller'.

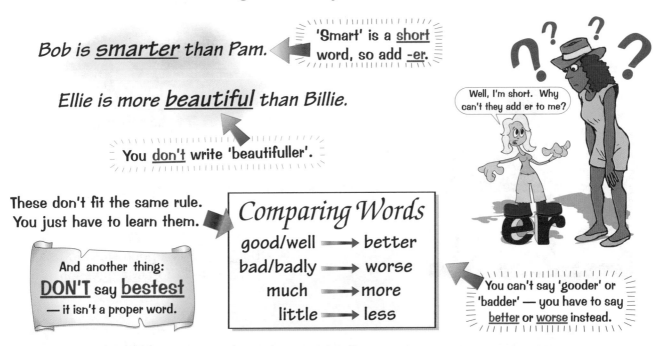

These don't fit the same rule. You just have to learn them.

Comparing Words

good/well → better
bad/badly → worse
much → more
little → less

And another thing: DON'T say bestest — it isn't a proper word.

You can't say 'gooder' or 'badder' — you have to say better or worse instead.

Writing about the Most — add -est to Short Words

Zzzoom!

Sometimes using '-er than' or 'more' isn't enough — you want to say that something is the best or worst, or the 'most' something. For short words, you can usually do this by adding '-est'.

It was the highest Chaz had ever jumped.

Use 'most' for Longer Words

For longer words, it doesn't sound right if you add '-est'. The thing to do is to use 'most', like here:

She's the most interesting chemistry teacher ever.

Don't EVER use 'most' and '-est' together
— don't say things like 'most prettiest' or 'most tallest'.

Comparing words? They're easy — more or less...

It does start to get a bit fiddly here — you need to sort out when to use 'more' and when to use '-er'... and never use both at the same time. It's the same for 'most' and '-est'.

Using Different Words

You can make a big difference to your work by using more interesting words.

Use Different words for 'Said'

Don't just write 'said' all the time. It's boring. You can use lots of different verbs to show when someone is speaking. Try some of these. They all have a different meaning.

"No, I don't want to arm wrestle," ***replied*** *Squirtina.*

Use 'replied' or 'answered' when someone answers.

"Are you a woman or a wimp?" ***demanded*** *Big Betty.*

'Demanded' is a good word to use for a really forceful question.

whispered	shouted	muttered	asked	replied
cried	yelled	repeated	commented	sobbed
complained	wailed	screamed	demanded	declared

"I was enjoying that!" ***wailed*** *Jim-Bob.*

Using 'wailed' tells you that he's speaking loudly and is upset.

"Bloomin' cowboys, they never learn," ***muttered*** *Mary-Lou.*

This lets you know that Mary-Lou was speaking very quietly.

Just get it learned — no need to wail and sob...

All you need to do is learn a few fancy ways of saying what someone's said. Practise using all these words till they've stuck fast in your head, then use them when you write.

Using Different Words

Don't use boring words like 'big' or 'nice' all the time. Here's how to come up with some better ones...

Look for Interesting Words when you Read

Whenever you're reading, you'll see loads of great words used instead of the usual boring ones.

The secret is to keep learning new words.
If you see a word that you don't understand when you're reading, find out what it means.

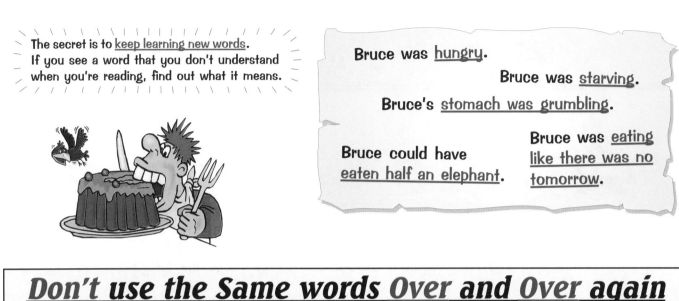

Bruce was hungry.

Bruce was starving.

Bruce's stomach was grumbling.

Bruce could have eaten half an elephant.

Bruce was eating like there was no tomorrow.

Don't use the Same words Over and Over again

Craig looked out to sea. He walked down to the edge of the sea and dipped his toes in the sea.

With 'sea' repeated like this it's boring.

Craig looked out to sea. He walked down to the shore and dipped his toes in the water.

This is so much better.

Nothing is Ever just 'Nice'

If you ever say that something is nice, you can bet that you could be a lot more interesting if you use a different word or phrase.

The film was...
- exciting
- brilliant
- scary, but I felt sorry for the villain at the end...

This new hairdo is...
- stunning
- as bright as a neon sign
- drop-dead gorgeous
- totally original

Don't repeat yourself...yourself...yourself...yourself...

It's so easy to use the same old words all the time. The thing is, the more you use them, the more of a habit it gets. Just giving the words you use a little thought will really improve your writing.

Sentences with 'and' and 'but'

You can put short sentences together to make longer ones.

1) Use 'and' to link Similar things

Hermes flew over Igor.

Nobby flew over Hermes.

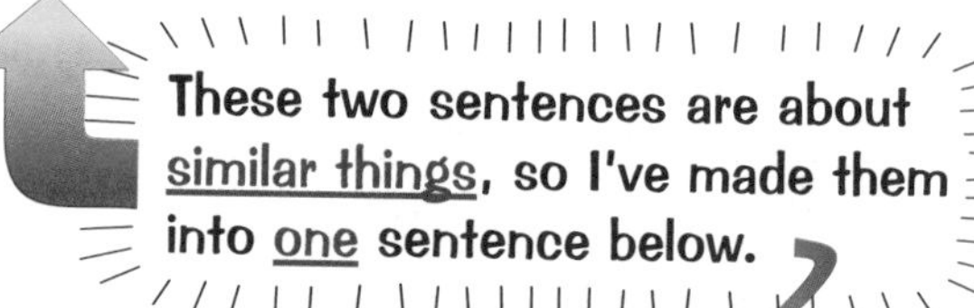

These two sentences are about similar things, so I've made them into one sentence below.

Hermes flew over Igor and Nobby flew over Hermes.

It's better in one sentence because it says that all the flying happened together.

2) Use 'but' to show Differences or Opposites

When you use 'but' to join two sentences, you're pointing out the difference between them.

This sentence makes the point that Sean and General Bob like different things.

Sean likes melon, but General Bob prefers monsters on toast.

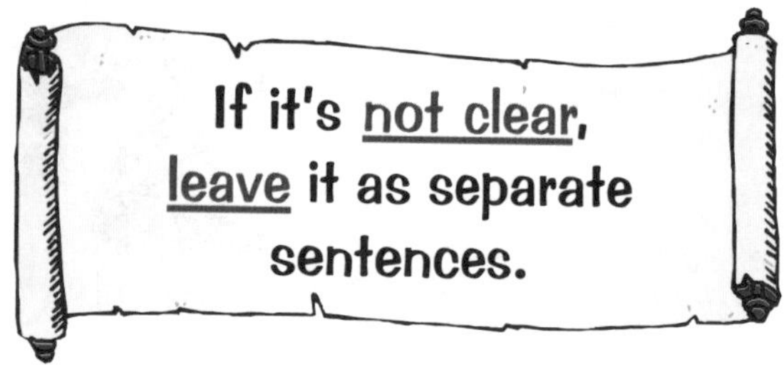

No pinching — get your 'ands off...

When you join two things together in a sentence, the sentence still has to be clear and easy to read. If it's not clear, either reword it or leave it as two separate sentences.

Don't Be Boring

Your sentences should be not too short, not too long, but just about right.

Don't Use 'And', 'And Then' and 'But' All the Time

And then I went to the gate and the guard let me in, and I asked to see the rest of the park, and he said, "Okay," and I went down a long path to where there was another building and I looked inside but it was empty.

MEGA BORING

This isn't just boring — it's confusing, too.

Once you've made a clear point, stop that sentence and start a new one.

It's much better to write separate sentences like this:

I went to the gate and the guard let me in. I asked to see the rest of the park and he said, "Okay." I went down a long path to where there was another building. I looked inside, but it was empty.

This looks much better. All I've done though is break it up into shorter sentences and take out some ands.

Don't Start all your Sentences the Same Way

This is an easy trap to get caught in, especially if you're not properly awake. Keep an eye on your writing, and remember to start your sentences in different ways.

Sid jumped out of the train. He hit the ground and rolled over the wet grass. He stood up carefully and looked at the countryside around him. He was safe at last.

Most of these sentences start with 'he'. It's very boring to read.

GO!
They're all starting differently!

This is a lot better. Changing the order of the words livens it up.

Sid jumped out of the train. He hit the ground and rolled over the wet grass. Carefully, he stood up and looked at the countryside around him. At last he was safe.

Drills — they sure know how to be boring...

'Don't be boring' sounds like a really obvious thing to say, but it's easy to lose your spark if you're not concentrating. Remember, how you write is as important as what you write.

Paragraphs Make Things Clear

Make sure you know how to use paragraphs — they make your writing much clearer.

Paragraphs Break Up Big Chunks of Text

Ending a paragraph gives you a pause for breath. It lets you have a little rest before you go on reading. Big chunks of text with no paragraphs leave you feeling breathless and exhausted.

The monster prowled through the streets, when suddenly it smelt food. The smell was coming from the house at the end of the road. The monster approached the front door in the light of the full moon.

There was a crash and Henry sat up in bed. He listened carefully, but the whole house was quiet. Nothing stirred in the darkness, and as Henry listened, he could hear the pounding of his own heartbeat.

Downstairs, the monster started to explore. It followed its nose towards the fridge in the kitchen. The smell was coming from the trifle Henry's mum had made. The monster gobbled it up.

Wrong — look at this great big chunk of text. It looks like it would be really hard work to read it all.

Right — this is the same text, split up into three paragraphs. It looks good and it's easier to read.

The monster prowled through the streets, when suddenly it smelt food. The smell was coming from the house at the end of the road. The monster approached the front door in the light of the full moon. There was a crash and Henry sat up in bed. He listened carefully, but the whole house was quiet. Nothing stirred in the darkness, and as Henry listened, he could hear the pounding of his own heartbeat. Downstairs, the monster started to explore. It followed its nose towards the fridge in the kitchen. The smell was coming from the trifle Henry's mum had made. The monster gobbled it up.

Put a Gap at the Start and Stop at the End

It's dead easy to write in paragraphs. First of all, remember to leave a gap before you write the first word.

Ending a paragraph is just as easy. You simply stop writing. After the last word of a paragraph, you leave the rest of that line blank.

Just a little gap — the size of a few letters

This is how you start a new paragraph. Just leave a little gap before you write the first word. To end a paragraph, you simply stop writing and leave the rest of the line blank.

The rest of this line is blank.

Paragraphs — they're the graphs in green berets...

It's dead important that you remember to break up your writing by using lots of paragraphs. If you keep rambling on, you end up with a long chunk of text that nobody will want to read.

Writing Paragraphs

It's not quite as simple as stopping every now and then and starting a new paragraph. It's almost that simple, but not quite. Paragraphs have to hang together.

All the Sentences in a Paragraph are Related

Look very carefully at the paragraphs in this story. Where the paragraphs are put in isn't just random. Each paragraph contains related sentences.

This paragraph is all about the monster before it gets into the house.

The monster prowled through the streets, when suddenly it smelt food. The smell was coming from the house at the end of the road. The monster approached the front door in the light of the full moon.

All these sentences are about Henry waking up and wondering what the noise is.

There was a crash and Henry sat up in bed. He listened carefully, but the whole house was quiet. Nothing stirred in the darkness, and as Henry listened, he could hear the pounding of his own heartbeat.

This paragraph is all about the monster when it's inside the house.

Downstairs, the monster started to explore. It followed its nose towards the fridge in the kitchen. The smell was coming from the trifle Henry's mum had made. The monster gobbled it up.

If you don't know when you should start a new paragraph, don't worry — I'll tell you on the next three pages. For the moment, just remember this rule:

How terribly kind, I do so love trifle

> Paragraphs are groups of sentences which go together — because they talk about the same thing, or because they follow on from each other.

Aunts, uncles, sentences — they're all related...

Paragraphs don't just make your writing look easier to read by breaking it up into smaller chunks. They're a really useful way of organising what you're saying — related sentences go together.

When to Start a New Paragraph

It's not always obvious when you should start a new paragraph — mostly it's common sense, and something that comes with practice. But learning the rules on these pages will help you.

Start a New Paragraph when Something Changes

This is the golden rule for paragraphs — you'd better learn it now.

When you write a story or a letter, you should start a new paragraph every time something changes.

Here are five types of things that could change. I'll explain each one in the next few pages:

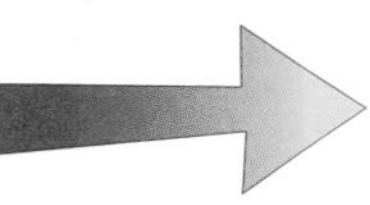

1) Something new happens
2) You talk about a new person
3) A new person speaks
4) You write about a different place
5) You move to a different time

1) When Something New happens

Whenever you talk about something new happening, you have to use a new paragraph.

These sentences are about Harry and Sam waiting and being bored, so they're in the same paragraph.

The buzzing is a new thing, so use a new paragraph.

The bees are a new thing, so use a new paragraph.

Harry and Sam had been waiting for ages. There was nothing to do, and there was nothing to look at. They were bored.

Suddenly they heard the buzzing. It started off so quietly they could hardly hear it, but it grew louder until it rang in their ears like a bell.

Then they saw the bees — huge, fierce things flying towards them like massive bullets. There were hundreds of them, all in a big swarm.

Count bird numbers — Use a New Parrot Graph...

There's just one thing to remember here, but it's dead important — each time you start writing about something new in your story or your letter, you must always start a new paragraph.

When to Start a New Paragraph

Here are two more uses for paragraphs — when you're writing a story, use a new paragraph every time you write about a new person and every time a person actually speaks.

2) When you Talk about a New Person

Up, up
and away!

Whenever a new person appears in your writing, you should start a new paragraph — it shows the reader that something has changed.

New paragraph to talk about Naomi.

Ryan swung his racket and smacked the ball up into the air. It flew up into the sky and then fell like a stone onto Naomi's head.

Naomi was normally a quiet, friendly girl. She had been watching the tennis match for five minutes or so, without saying anything. When the ball hit her, though, she burst into tears.

3) Each time a Person Speaks

I'm sorry,
he made
me do it

When you write a story, it's important to put in sentences where the people involved actually say or think something.

Every time someone starts speaking, you start a new paragraph.

That includes when one person stops talking, and someone else starts.

Alison is actually speaking so start a new paragraph.

When the same person keeps on talking, you don't have to start a new paragraph.

Here the speakers change so you start new paragraphs.

The fisherman was sitting in his boat when Alison came to the end of the jetty.

"Have you caught anything?" she asked.

"I haven't caught a thing all day," growled the fisherman crossly. He was busy mending his nets.

"Better luck tomorrow!" replied Alison. "You never know what you might catch then. Maybe a shark!"

"There aren't any sharks around here," said the fisherman.

"What's that then?" asked Alison, pointing to the big blue fin in the water.

Count rabbit food — Use a New Carrot Graph...

You have to start a new paragraph when you start talking about someone new, and when someone starts speaking. If you wrote that fisherman story in one big long chunk, it'd be very hard to read.

When to Start a New Paragraph

When you write about a new place or a new time, you have to start a new paragraph.

4) When you Write about a Different Place

Every time the story or letter moves to another place, you need to start a new paragraph.

This helps the reader to see that you're writing about something different.

This paragraph is about the jungle.

An elephant standing on its trunk — how ridiculous.

The elephants were stampeding through the jungle. They knocked down trees left and right, and all the other animals were running for their lives.

Back in the village, Adele was doing her homework when the ground began to shake.

This is about the village so it's a new paragraph.

5) When the Story or Letter Moves to a Different Time

Sometimes a story or a letter moves in time. It can go backwards or forwards to talk about something that happened at a different time.

Whenever the story or letter moves in time, you should start a new paragraph.

Each paragraph talks about a different time.

Today I went to school, and it was a boring day. It was raining at break time so we weren't allowed outside.

Yesterday it was really sunny, though. The weather was so nice we went outside to do a class experiment in the wild area.

It was late so we decided to go home.

The next day we got up early. We wanted to see if we could catch the goblins dancing in the forest before dawn.

This has gone forward to a different time.

Revise paragraphs — this is the time and the place...

So, five times when you have to change paragraphs are when — 1) something new happens, 2) you talk about a new person, 3) someone speaks, 4) you write about a different place, or 5) you move to a different time. Remember these and your writing will be much easier to read.

Revision Summary for Sections 3 & 4

Dull, dull, dull. Yep, I reckon so too. But it's not really hard, and once you've learnt it, you'll do tons better at English. After all, if you don't learn all this stuff about sentences and paragraphs, you won't be able to write properly. Try all of these questions, then go back over the section and look up any you can't do...

1) What are doing and being words called?
2) Should every sentence have: a) a verb, or b) a reference to a freak yodelling accident?
3) Correct this sentence: I swum across the pool, but my shorts shrunk so I hid at the deep end.
4) Correct this sentence: I've broke the record — I've laid here all day without moving.
5) When you add '-ing' to a word, when should you double the last letter of the word?
6) What do you do when you add '-ing' to a word that ends in 'e'?
7) Make these verbs talk about the past: deal, laugh, weep, kick, mean, creep, burn, learn, stop.
8) Rewrite this sentence, but add in some describing words to make it more interesting:
   The man walked from his house to the rocket.
9) What's a metaphor?
10) Give five examples of words that sound a bit like what they mean (onomatopoeia).
11) When should you add -er to a word to mean more?
    How can you make these mean more of whatever: tall, green, intelligent, bright-eyed, rich, pretty?
12) When should you add -est to a word to mean most?
    How can you make these words mean the most of whatever: tall, intelligent, bat-shaped, red?
13) Put some more interesting words in these sentences instead of 'said':
    "Come here!" said the furious teacher. "No, thanks," said Reginald.
    "I hope he doesn't hear us," said Harold to the spy. "Arggh!" said the spy.
14) Write these bits of writing again, but change the boring repeating words:
    Kate looked down at her cat. The cat wanted to be taken for a walk. Kate sighed, went to the cat's cupboard and got out the cat's collar and lead. "You're a really daft cat," she murmured. "You always think you're a dog."
15) And the same for this:
    Dennis ran down the street. The street was hard beneath his feet, which were starting to hurt. He walked barefoot down this street every day, but now he was being chased by the burglar he'd discovered robbing a house at the end of the street.
16) Make these sentences more interesting by replacing the boring word 'nice':
    Fred's new computer game is nice. My hat is nice. This book is nice. The cocktails were nice.
17) Use 'and' and 'but' to turn these pairs of sentences into single sentences:
    a) Sharon bought one hundred and eighty apples. Shirley bought three hundred bananas.
    b) Keith likes the new song by Stairs. Mick hates it.
18) Write this out again, but use the word 'and' less:
    I entered an underwater-basket-weaving competition and I made a really cool basket and it was made of red straw and it looked far better than any other basket I've ever made and I came third.
19) How do you start a new paragraph? How do you end it?
20) Should all the sentences in a paragraph be:
    a) about completely different stuff, b) related, c) about Portuguese trees. a, b or c?
21) You should start a new paragraph every time something changes. List five types of change that mean you should start a new paragraph.

Improving Your Handwriting

If your handwriting looks like splodgy spider trails then no one will be able to read it.

Handwriting is Important

There are two big problems if your handwriting is too messy to read.

1. Your teacher might miss out on some of your brilliant points.
2. No one will be able to tell if you're spelling things correctly.

REMEMBER

What YOU have to say IS IMPORTANT.
So you'd better make sure people can read it.

Don't be Fancy, just be Neat

It's not a good plan to be really fancy with your writing.

Hey Tim, "Simple and Neat Man..."
"Simple is Sweet!"

Don't muck about with fancy curly bits.
Don't put circles above the letter i — just dots.

Keep it simple and keep it neat.

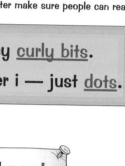

Too much fancy stuff will bring you unstuck every time.

Get your Spacing Right

There are two things to watch out for.

Make sure everything is in the right place when you write...
...and make sure each word is neat on its own.

Make sure the spaces between your words are all the same size.

Keep your writing on the line.
Don't let it float above or below.

If your writing does float off, it'll look scruffy, it'll be harder to read, and it might get tangled up in the line above or below. That's bad news. So don't let it happen.

Be neat — like gin without tonic...

If no one can read what you write, there's no point writing anything. So keep it clear. That means no fancy curly bits. Keep the writing on the line, and the spaces between words the same size.

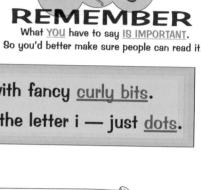

Improving Your Handwriting

It's no good just planning to write neatly in the exams. You need to get in the habit of writing neatly all the time. Learn these four steps to handwriting heaven, and practise them.

Four Really Useful Handwriting Hints

1. Make sure that your capital letters are bigger than your ordinary letters.

2. Small letters like a,c,e and s should all be the same height.

3. Tall letters like l, k and f are almost as tall as capital letters, but not quite — do them about twice as tall as a small letter. The letter t is halfway between a small letter and a tall letter.

PRINTING

Lpdyt

OR

HANDWRITING

Lpdyt

The Rules are the same for both.

IMPORTANT... make sure you can READ WHAT YOU HAVE WRITTEN. Or you'll just lose silly marks.

dlb dlb dlb

In each of these all of the letters go in the same direction, so they're fine.

dlb ← These go in different directions, they're wrong.

4. Letters that stick up or down like l, d, y and g should all slant the same way or go straight up or down.

What to Do if you make a Mistake

If you make a mistake with spelling, put two lines through the word and put brackets around it. Then write what you meant to write above the mistake.

Do it like this.

messy

Don't be (~~mesy~~) when you write.

Don't keep scribbling it out until there's a big splodge over it — that looks awful.

Handwriting — nothing like finger-painting...

Making your letters the right size and shape is crucial if you want to have good handwriting. Do your small letters all the same size, taller letters about twice as big, and bigger still for capitals.

Spelling — Two Great Tips

The right letters in the right order — that's all there is to it...

You Can Learn to Spell

I'm still learning to spell
L

You can't get away with bad spelling. It makes you look bad, your writing is hard to read, and you'll get marked down.

The good news is nobody spells everything wrong.

For words you can't spell, there are little tricks and rhymes to help you get them right. Concentrate on the hard words, use your tricks and you'll be word perfect in no time.

Two Great Spelling Tips

Long words are often made up of smaller words put together. Keep an eye out for this — it makes them a whole lot easier to spell.

Morris — set this in stone...
BREAK WORDS INTO CHUNKS
King U-Can-Spell

Inside = in + side

Careless = care + less

Handwriting = hand + writing

Be careful, though, words that end in -ful are different. Care + full → careful. The second letter l is always dropped.

Use + full → useful

Hope + full → hopeful

Success + full → successful

If you can break up the word into chunks, it makes it loads easier to spell.

Careful mate — you've dropped an 'l'...

Spelling really is important — for one thing, you'll never find things on the Internet if you can't spell. Think about long words made up of smaller ones, and remember to drop that last 'l' from '-full'.

Spelling Words with 'ie' or 'ei'

The i Before e Rule

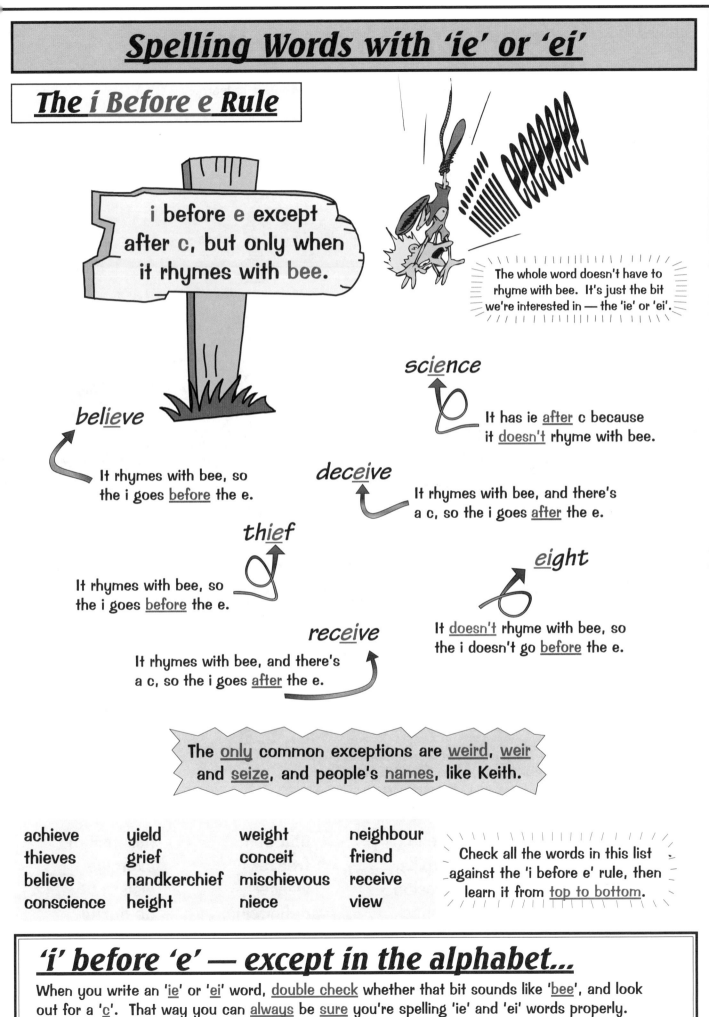

i before e except after c, but only when it rhymes with bee.

The whole word doesn't have to rhyme with bee. It's just the bit we're interested in — the 'ie' or 'ei'.

science — It has ie after c because it doesn't rhyme with bee.

believe — It rhymes with bee, so the i goes before the e.

deceive — It rhymes with bee, and there's a c, so the i goes after the e.

thief — It rhymes with bee, so the i goes before the e.

eight — It doesn't rhyme with bee, so the i doesn't go before the e.

receive — It rhymes with bee, and there's a c, so the i goes after the e.

The only common exceptions are weird, weir and seize, and people's names, like Keith.

achieve	yield	weight	neighbour
thieves	grief	conceit	friend
believe	handkerchief	mischievous	receive
conscience	height	niece	view

Check all the words in this list against the 'i before e' rule, then learn it from top to bottom.

'i' before 'e' — except in the alphabet...

When you write an 'ie' or 'ei' word, double check whether that bit sounds like 'bee', and look out for a 'c'. That way you can always be sure you're spelling 'ie' and 'ei' words properly.

Difficult and Tricky Words

Sorry, but some words have awkward spellings that you just have to learn...

You Have to Learn these words

These words are plain tricky. Their spelling isn't the same as the way they sound. The only thing to do is learn them all.

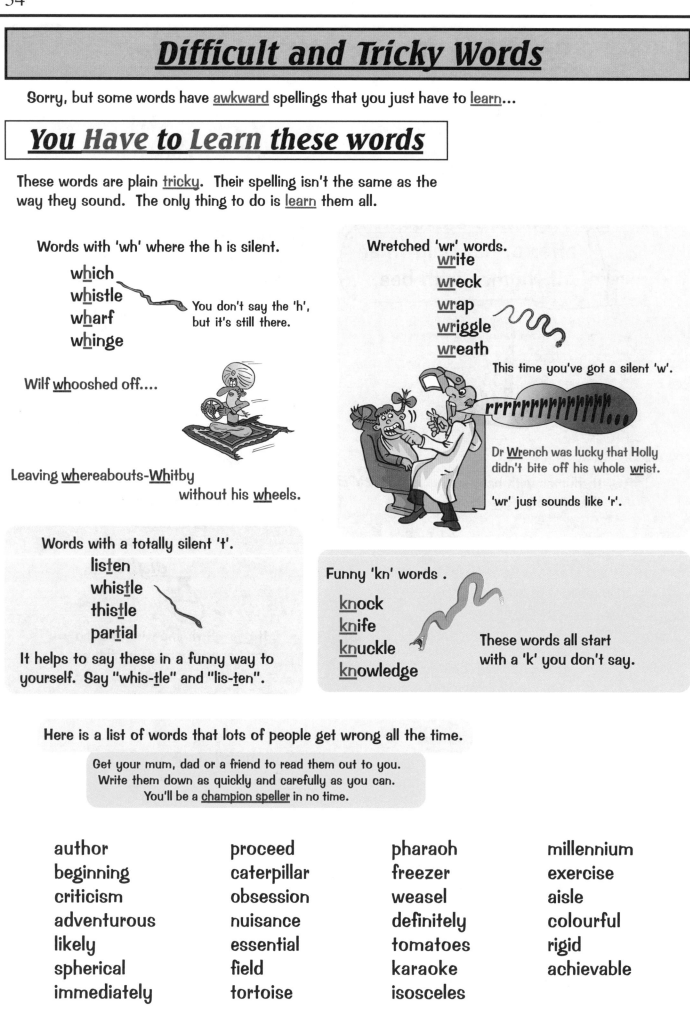

Words with 'wh' where the h is silent.

which
whistle
wharf
whinge

You don't say the 'h', but it's still there.

Wilf whooshed off....

Leaving whereabouts-Whitby without his wheels.

Wretched 'wr' words.

write
wreck
wrap
wriggle
wreath

This time you've got a silent 'w'.

Dr Wrench was lucky that Holly didn't bite off his whole wrist.

'wr' just sounds like 'r'.

Words with a totally silent 't'.

listen
whistle
thistle
partial

It helps to say these in a funny way to yourself. Say "whis-tle" and "lis-ten".

Funny 'kn' words .

knock
knife
knuckle
knowledge

These words all start with a 'k' you don't say.

Here is a list of words that lots of people get wrong all the time.

Get your mum, dad or a friend to read them out to you.
Write them down as quickly and carefully as you can.
You'll be a champion speller in no time.

author	proceed	pharaoh	millennium
beginning	caterpillar	freezer	exercise
criticism	obsession	weasel	aisle
adventurous	nuisance	definitely	colourful
likely	essential	tomatoes	rigid
spherical	field	karaoke	achievable
immediately	tortoise	isosceles	

Difficult and Tricky Words

I know I've said this before, but to be good at this spelling thing you must go over it again and again.

Sounding out words can help you spell them

Rotten 'r'.

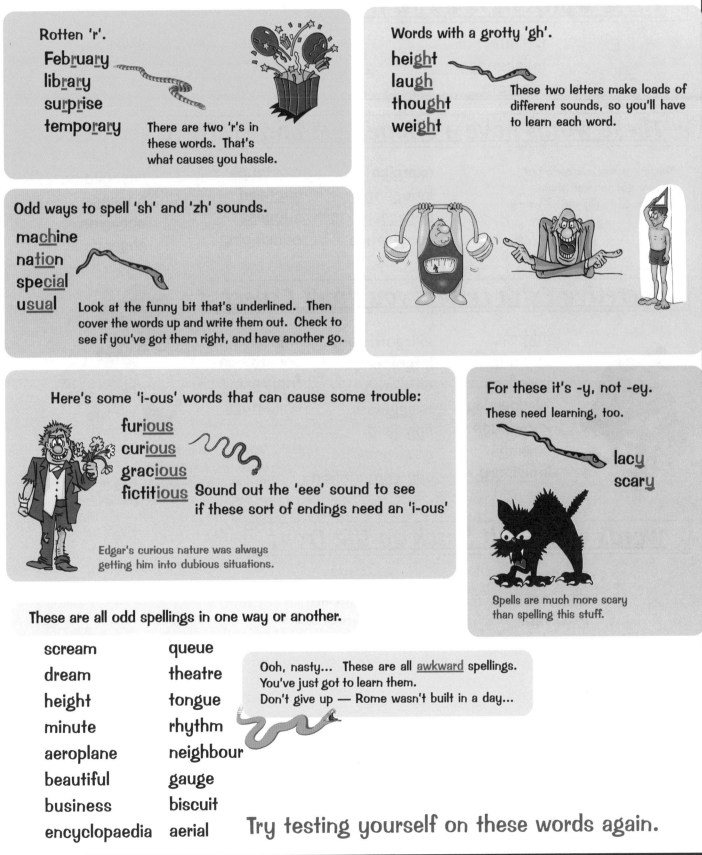

February
library
surprise
temporary

There are two 'r's in these words. That's what causes you hassle.

Words with a grotty 'gh'.

height
laugh
thought
weight

These two letters make loads of different sounds, so you'll have to learn each word.

Odd ways to spell 'sh' and 'zh' sounds.

machine
nation
special
usual

Look at the funny bit that's underlined. Then cover the words up and write them out. Check to see if you've got them right, and have another go.

Here's some 'i-ous' words that can cause some trouble:

furious
curious
gracious
fictitious

Sound out the 'eee' sound to see if these sort of endings need an 'i-ous'

Edgar's curious nature was always getting him into dubious situations.

For these it's -y, not -ey.

These need learning, too.

lacy
scary

Spells are much more scary than spelling this stuff.

These are all odd spellings in one way or another.

scream	queue
dream	theatre
height	tongue
minute	rhythm
aeroplane	neighbour
beautiful	gauge
business	biscuit
encyclopaedia	aerial

Ooh, nasty... These are all awkward spellings. You've just got to learn them. Don't give up — Rome wasn't built in a day...

Try testing yourself on these words again.

Difficult and Tricky Words

Just when you thought it was safe to turn the page — here are some more words you need to know.

Learn how to Spell All These Words

These words have awkward vowels

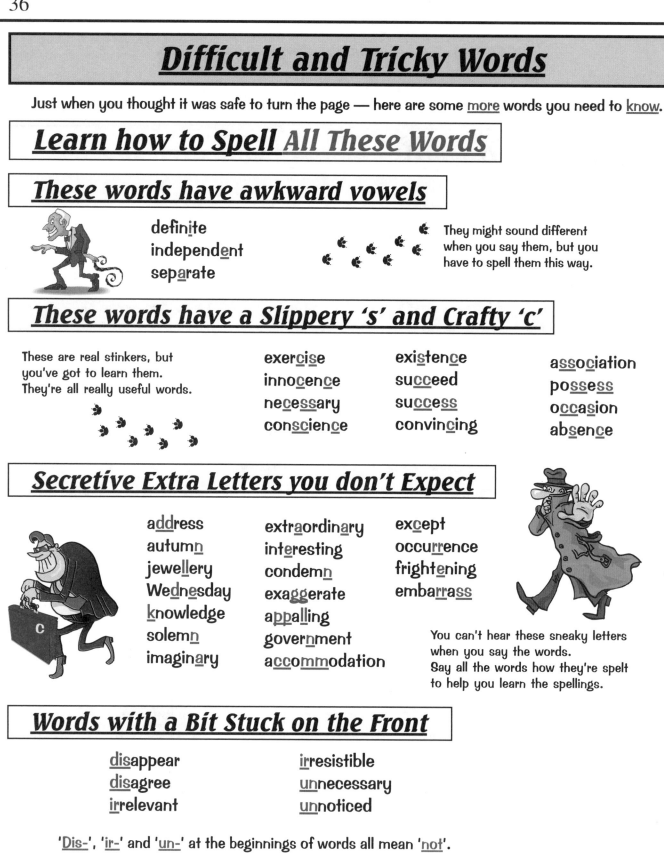

definite
independent
separate

They might sound different when you say them, but you have to spell them this way.

These words have a Slippery 's' and Crafty 'c'

These are real stinkers, but you've got to learn them. They're all really useful words.

exercise
innocence
necessary
conscience

existence
succeed
success
convincing

association
possess
occasion
absence

Secretive Extra Letters you don't Expect

address
autumn
jewellery
Wednesday
knowledge
solemn
imaginary

extraordinary
interesting
condemn
exaggerate
appalling
government
accommodation

except
occurrence
frightening
embarrass

You can't hear these sneaky letters when you say the words.
Say all the words how they're spelt to help you learn the spellings.

Words with a Bit Stuck on the Front

disappear
disagree
irrelevant

irresistible
unnecessary
unnoticed

'Dis-', 'ir-' and 'un-' at the beginnings of words all mean 'not'.

If you remember the original word when you write the 'not' word, it should be easier to spell.

Words with a sneaky Letter 'e'

ninety
likeable
loveable

Ooh, but this letter 'e' is easy to forget. It's part of the original words — 'nine', 'like' and 'love' — so don't miss it out.

Looking at the Question

It's always tempting to start writing straight away, but it's really not a good idea...

Read the Question

Right, so you've been set a question. Before you start writing, read what you've been asked to do. Make sure you know what you're supposed to write about.

If there's a choice of questions, <u>don't</u> just pick the first one. It might not be the easiest.

Think First

Write in the Style the Question Tells You

Always think about what kind of writing the question is asking you to do. This has to do with who you are — the question may ask you to imagine you're a teacher, or a character in a story. You have to think what words they would use to write or say something.

Say the question tells you to imagine you're a character in a story. Then you have to write in the kind of way that character would write.

Philip stood in the museum looking at the dinosaur bones. There was a sign saying "do not touch", but Philip didn't see it. After a while he reached out and grabbed hold of a bone. The museum attendant quickly ran over and told him to stop.

Q1. Imagine you are the museum attendant. Write an account of the same event.

You should write the way he or she would write — use some long and complicated words.

Remember that you might be angry about children mucking around in the museum.

Focus on the Question

Children have no respect for the rules of the museum. Only today I had to stop a young boy from touching the dinosaur bones.

Also look at who you're writing to — it may be a stranger, a friend, the readers of a magazine. You'd use a different style when writing to a friend than you would when writing for a magazine.

Forget the hocus pocus and focus on the question...

It may sound an obvious thing to say, but reading the question carefully is incredibly important. No matter how good your answer is, if it doesn't do what the question tells you, you're in deep trouble.

Planning Your Answer

People often get the idea that they're not much good at English when the only thing they get wrong is not thinking before they start writing. Learn to do it.

Plan Before you Start Writing

If you dive straight in without planning first, it'll all go horribly wrong.

All your writing needs a plan, whether you're doing homework, coursework or an exam.

One page of well planned, well thought out writing is always better than five pages written out of the top of your head.

A Plan Makes Writing Easier

A good plan is a whole lot more than a set of vague, kind-of-quite-good notes.
A plan tells you where your writing is going to go, so you don't get lost on the way.
Writing is much easier when you know what you're doing.

Decide what you want to say. Decide what order you want to put your points in.
Write down your main points in order.

Remember to use any suggestions in the question.
They make writing a plan so much easier.

Write quick notes about each of these things in this order. This is your plan.

Write about how you think old people should be treated by their families and in the community.

In your answer you could:

- explain some of the ways in which old people are treated;
- describe your experience of old people;
- say how you think old people should be treated by their families;
- say how you think old people should be treated by the community.

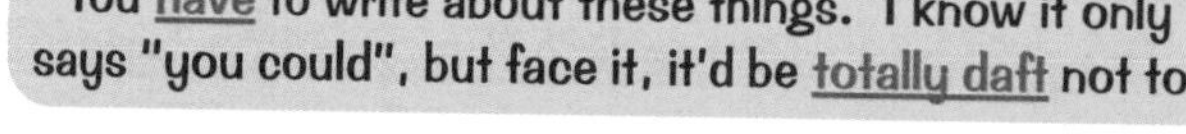

You have to write about these things. I know it only says "you could", but face it, it'd be totally daft not to.

Writing Essays

Have no fear — essays aren't a problem as long as you keep your head and remember the basics.

Essays Aren't Scary

The word 'essay' sounds a bit scary. People tend to think that there's some great secret to writing essays — but it's just not true.

It's half past three.
ESSAY

An Essay is a piece of writing that answers a question.

A simple yes or no might answer the question — but it won't get you many marks — you need to explain why.

Three Steps to Essay Heaven

1. Think of some points to do with the question. See if you can use them to answer the question, then work out what order to put them in. This is your plan.
2. Style is important — write clearly and try to sound intelligent. Use posh clever-sounding words if you can, but only if you know what they mean.
3. Write about each point one at a time. When you write the essay, start a new paragraph each time you start a new point. That automatically gets you better marks.

If you get an essay to write that isn't a direct question, turn it into a question:

Write an essay about your favourite sport.

Turn the essay into this question.

Why is your favourite sport good to play and fun to watch?

Rollerblading Stunt Hamster Races
Make Way! Coming through...

All you have to do is think of reasons why it's a good sport for people to play, and write about them. Think of reasons why it's fun to watch, and write about them, too.

My favourite sport: Rollerblading Stunt Hamster Races

Writing Stories

Personal writing means stories. They can be about things that have really happened to you, or they can be made up. Story writing is harder than you'd think, so it needs thought.

Plan Your Story — Who, What and Where

① Work out what's going to happen.

Harold loses his pig. He puts up 'Lost Pig' notices. He gives the pig up for lost and gets a dog to replace it. He takes the dog for a walk in the park and sees someone else walking the pig he lost in the first place.

Don't try to write a really long story in an exam — you don't have time. You'll end up rushing the ending.

② Work out who is involved in the story.

Harold Hebblethwaite and the lady walking his pig.

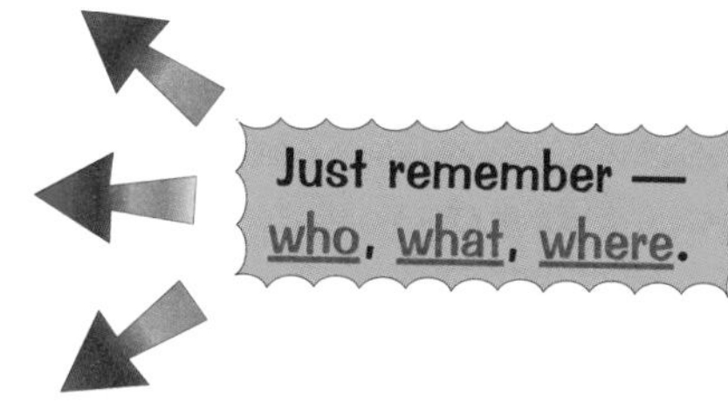
Just remember —
who, what, where.

③ Choose where it's going to happen.

Outside Harold's house and in the park.

A story needs a beginning, a middle and an end.

Beginning: Harold looking for the pig.
Middle: Putting up the notices, giving up and getting a dog.
End: Seeing the pig in the park — agreeing to swap pets?

Planning a 'Write about a time when...' Story

Write about a time when you wish you had acted differently.

Think about things that you've been through, or things that you've done. Pick one where you felt the same as the question says.

Write about how you felt as well as what happened.

The time when I let a friend borrow my brother's bike and he ended up wrecking it.
How I felt: worried — but I let my mate take it anyway, guilty when he brought back the trashed bike, scared of my brother and really stupid.

How on Earth? — just planet...

Planning means thinking about what you're going to write before you start. You'll do yourself no favours if you just a scribble down a few quick lines. Make sure you really plan it properly.

How to Start a Story

No one wants to read a story with a boring start — and that includes your teacher. The beginning needs to GRAB THE READER'S ATTENTION.

Start with something Exciting

Start with something exciting, and the person reading your story can't help but want to read on. They'll want to find out what happens next.

Naomi moved away. The edge of the cliff crumbled and she plunged backwards.

If you start with someone speaking, the person reading your story will want to find out who they are and what they're talking about.

"Be careful with those marshmallows!" shouted John, but it was no use. Tim had decided that he was going to take his marshmallows to the moon, and there was no stopping him.

The first line of your story can tell you about what is happening. Don't explain everything at once. Make the reader want to read on.

Make Sure it's Clear Who 'She' is

When you use 'he' and 'she' to write about your main characters, watch out.

Super Salami Girl took a deep breath, preparing for the confrontation, and threw herself through Evil Zyra's window. She looked up and saw her standing there.

Don't let this happen — you can't tell whether Evil Zyra saw Super Salami Girl, or Super Salami Girl saw Evil Zyra.

Super Salami Girl stood and took careful aim with her fork... There was no hope for Evil Zyra — her time had come...

History, her story — everyone has a story to tell...

Concentrate on getting your readers hooked. Don't let it get confusing — make it clear who you're talking about. Make your start gripping and keep your readers gagging for more. Simple really.

Writing a Formal Letter

For your test, you may be given a chance to write a letter, either a formal or an informal one. Formal letters follow a strict set of rules, which are shown in blue in the letter below. Look at the letter and learn the rules for writing them:

Address of the person you are writing to.

Your address.

1 Bubbly Lane
Waterford
WA3 6PP
4/10/99

Date — day/month/year.

Mrs V Suddy-Waters
Managing Director
Space Age Washing Machines PLC
Huyton
HU5 7EZ

If you don't know their name, just put "Dear Sir/Madam".

Dear Mrs Suddy-Waters,

Put what the letter is about here.

Re: Performance of your washing machines

The first bit gives your reason for writing.

I am writing to complain about the standard and performance of my week-old space-age turbo-boosted washing machine. Having read a rave review of said machine in Washing Appliances Monthly I was eager to try out my new machine — until I switched it on.

Space to make it easier for people to read the letter.

When I turned it on the machine made a high-pitched whining coupled with a deep, low, rumbling groan. After approximately five minutes the whole machine began to vibrate violently, sending tremors through my kitchen. This caused the antique crystal chandelier to fall from the ceiling and shatter.

Clear paragraphs for each point.

At this point I attempted to phone your company's help desk. I was left on hold for thirty minutes listening to Whigfield's greatest hits whilst waiting for an operator to speak to me.

When I returned to the kitchen I found to my horror that my new washing machine had begun to froth around the door and foam was escaping across the kitchen floor. I turned it off and began to tidy up. At the very least I would like a full refund and the removal of the machine as soon as possible.

Formal language.

I hope that you will resolve this matter immediately so that I am not forced to take further action and contact Watch Hog.

Yours sincerely,

AS Cool

Ms Alia Cool

To end — use "Yours sincerely" when you know the person's name. If you've put "Dear Sir/Madam" at the top, then put "Yours faithfully" here.

Your signature, with your full name below it. Put 'Mr', 'Ms' or 'Miss' before your name.

Using Formal Language

Formal letters have to look right — but that's not all. If you want to get it right, you'd better use the right sort of words. Read on and all will be revealed...

Use Formal Language in a Formal Letter

When you write a formal letter, you don't just have to make sure it looks right. You have to use the right type of language as well. Formal language can be a bit tricky.

Formal language is the sort that's used in the letters you take home from school. It often doesn't sound like it's talking directly to someone. It says what should happen and what needs to be done instead of telling you directly to do something. It also often uses longer words...

Look Miss, I've written a letter.
A

1. Instead of writing *'I got'* ✗
   write *'I received'*. ✓

2. Instead of writing *'We want you to...'* ✗
   write *'It is expected that you will...'* ✓

3. Instead of writing *'Please write to or phone Mr Smith'* ✗
   write *'Please contact Mr Smith.'* ✓

4. Instead of writing *'When you're in the museum, you must be quiet'* ✗
   write *'Visitors are requested to remain silent'*. ✓

5. Also, don't use shortened words like *'can't'*, *'won't'* and *'TV'*. ✗
   Write them out in full as *'cannot'*, *'will not'* and *'television'*. ✓

Don't use Exclamation Marks

Formal language doesn't use exclamation marks. You can write polite questions — remember that these need question marks. Make sure that your questions are polite.

Formal lettuce — a well dressed salad...

Remember — formal language is what's used in the letters that you get from school (well, most of them anyway). Look at loads of them, and compare them to the stuff on this page. The more you look at, the more the facts will lodge themselves in your brain. Soon it will all seem so easy...

Writing an Informal Letter

If you're writing to a friend or someone else you know very well, then you can write an informal letter. Informal letters are much more friendly, and you don't have to bother with all the fancy formal language like on the last page. Take a look at this letter...

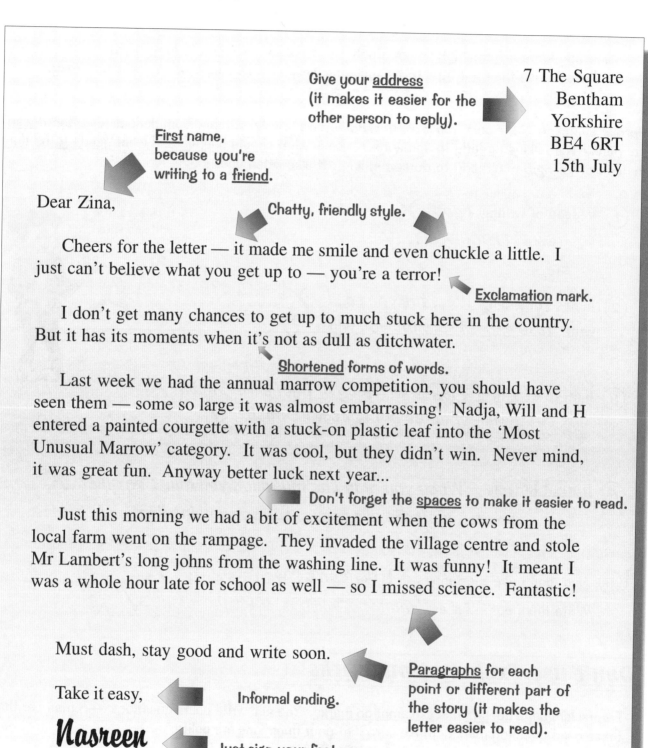

Give your address (it makes it easier for the other person to reply).

7 The Square
Bentham
Yorkshire
BE4 6RT
15th July

First name, because you're writing to a friend.

Dear Zina,

Chatty, friendly style.

Cheers for the letter — it made me smile and even chuckle a little. I just can't believe what you get up to — you're a terror!

Exclamation mark.

I don't get many chances to get up to much stuck here in the country. But it has its moments when it's not as dull as ditchwater.

Shortened forms of words.

Last week we had the annual marrow competition, you should have seen them — some so large it was almost embarrassing! Nadja, Will and H entered a painted courgette with a stuck-on plastic leaf into the 'Most Unusual Marrow' category. It was cool, but they didn't win. Never mind, it was great fun. Anyway better luck next year...

Don't forget the spaces to make it easier to read.

Just this morning we had a bit of excitement when the cows from the local farm went on the rampage. They invaded the village centre and stole Mr Lambert's long johns from the washing line. It was funny! It meant I was a whole hour late for school as well — so I missed science. Fantastic!

Must dash, stay good and write soon.

Paragraphs for each point or different part of the story (it makes the letter easier to read).

Take it easy,

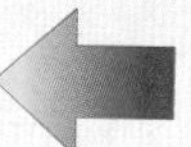

Informal ending.

Nasreen

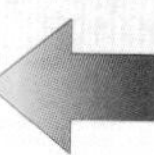

Just sign your first name.

Using Chatty Language

It should be a piece of cake writing these friendly letters...that doesn't mean you can get out of thinking them over thoroughly and using proper sentences. Here's how to do it...

Informal Letters use casual Chatty Language

1. Pretend you're talking to the person you're writing to and write the letter as you'd speak it — it'll sound more natural.
2. Proper sentences are still a must, even though you want to write in a friendly way — without them you'll lose bucket-loads of marks.
3. Have a look at the last page — it's fine to use shortened words like 'can't', 'won't' and 'didn't' — and exclamation marks!
4. Look back at the formal letter and try to compare it with the informal one to see the differences.

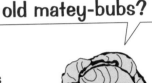

How's it goin' me old matey-bubs?

Informal Lettuce

Whatever the Type of letter — always Plan it...

1. Planning a letter is just as important as planning a story or an essay. If you don't plan it out first, you won't do the best job that you possibly can.
2. Jot down the main points that you want to make in the letter. Don't try to say too much or you won't have time to write it all.
3. But remember — if the question gives you ideas and points that you have to include, you must put them all in.

...and get that Layout right

Informal letters still need to have the address in the right place, but you don't need to finish with *'Yours sincerely'*. Just end with *'See you soon'*, *'Please write back!'*, *'Cheers, mate'* *'Take care'*, or anything that shows you're writing to someone you know.

Inform all lettuce — salad eaters approaching...

You'd think it would be easy to be informal, but there's lots of trickly little things to watch out for. The hard bit is making it sound like you're talking to them, but still using proper sentences.

Writing a Magazine Article

Articles in magazines often try to persuade people of a point of view.

Plan your Writing First

You need to think about what you're going to write, come up with some ideas for your answer and work out what order you're going to put them in.

Write an article for the school magazine on a topic you feel strongly about.

You can choose absolutely anything that you really feel strongly about. Try to convince everybody to agree with you.

I always planet — it's the only way to go!
Remember to plan it

Young people are more lazy than ever.
Write an article agreeing or disagreeing with this statement.

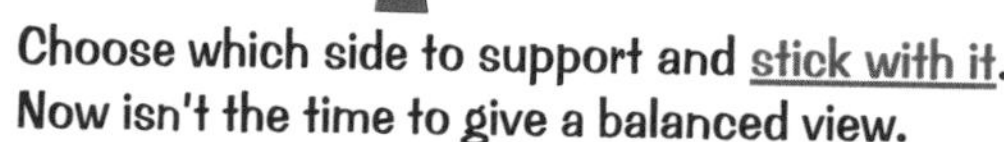

Choose which side to support and stick with it. Now isn't the time to give a balanced view.

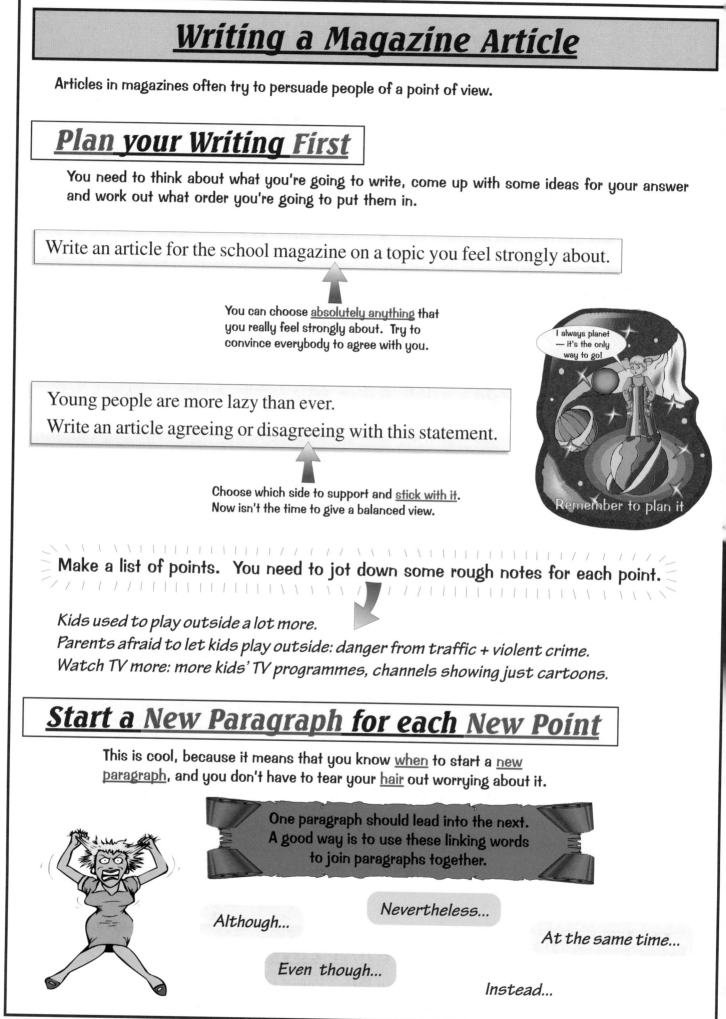

Make a list of points. You need to jot down some rough notes for each point.

Kids used to play outside a lot more.
Parents afraid to let kids play outside: danger from traffic + violent crime.
Watch TV more: more kids' TV programmes, channels showing just cartoons.

Start a New Paragraph for each New Point

This is cool, because it means that you know when to start a new paragraph, and you don't have to tear your hair out worrying about it.

One paragraph should lead into the next. A good way is to use these linking words to join paragraphs together.

Although...

Nevertheless...

At the same time...

Even though...

Instead...

Writing a Magazine Article

You've got to sell your point of view — just like an advert sells a product and persuades you to buy it. Learn these tricks and use them when you have to write persuasively.

You Can Exaggerate to Stress a Point

Exaggerating means making something out to be more than it really is.

Our diet is killing us.

You don't really mean that people are dropping dead every day.

You're just saying that the food we eat is bad for us.

Everyone knows that fast food is bad for you.

Making your point out to be a simple fact that everyone knows is another good trick.

But don't be rude:

If you eat burgers and chips, you must be a nutcase.

If people think you're attacking them, they won't want to listen to you.

Talk about 'Us' — Make your Writing Personal

This is an issue that affects us all.

People reading your article will know that you're talking about them as well as yourself.

Using questions is another useful trick. Politicians do it all the time in their speeches.

Do we want to eat food covered in poison?

Leave it to the readers to give the answer in their heads, instead of saying it yourself.

Use exaggerated language like "covered in poison". It tells the readers what your opinion really is. They'll answer the question in the way you want them to.

Make a painter laugh — write an art tickle...

OK, there are two major ways to make your articles more persuasive: 1) Remember to exaggerate — but whatever you do, don't be rude. 2) Make it personal — use words like 'we', 'our' and 'us'. Think about how someone else would react when they read it.

How to End Your Writing

A good piece of writing needs a good ending. Writing that just stops suddenly leaves your readers disappointed.

Ending a Story

Think about the ending before you start. A good ending ties up the loose ends of the story. The reader shouldn't be left thinking "I don't understand what happened".

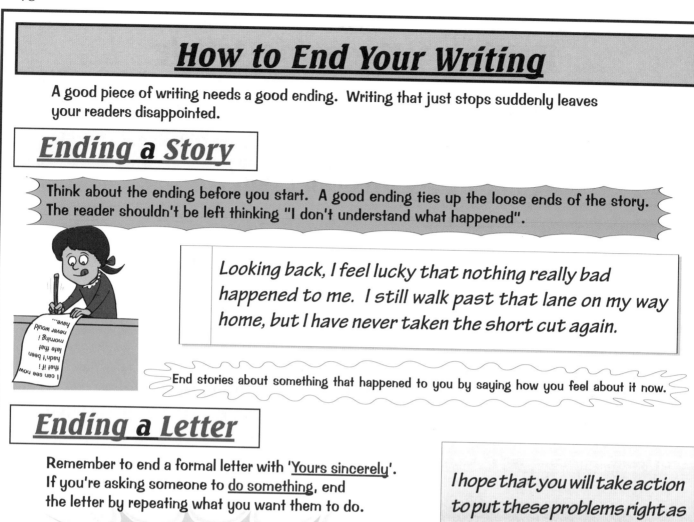

Looking back, I feel lucky that nothing really bad happened to me. I still walk past that lane on my way home, but I have never taken the short cut again.

End stories about something that happened to you by saying how you feel about it now.

Ending a Letter

Remember to end a formal letter with 'Yours sincerely'. If you're asking someone to do something, end the letter by repeating what you want them to do.

This is a good ending for a letter of complaint. It reminds the reader that they're supposed to do something about the complaint.

I hope that you will take action to put these problems right as soon as possible.
Yours sincerely...

We hope that you will wish to take us up on this amazing offer. Our telephone sales staff are waiting for your call.
Yours sincerely...

This is a good ending for a letter written to sell something. It ends by telling readers to buy it straightaway.

Ending a Persuasive Article

The clever bit here is linking the end of the article to something you've said at the beginning.

The lack of facilities provided by local authorities for the new craze sport, Rollerblading Stunt Hamster Races, is an issue which affects us all.

This in indeed an issue that affects us all, and we all have the power to do something about it. Please petition your local MP today.

Use the same words as the beginning.

Ask the readers to do something.

Revision Summary for Sections 5 & 6

OK. Now you know all about how to make your handwriting look great, how to spell and how to write well. But the only way you can really learn it is to practise. And a great way to practise is to do these questions. Don't worry if you can't do them all straight off — look back at the section to find the answer. But come back to the questions after a while and check you can do them all. Check them tomorrow. And next week. And next month. If you can still do them then, you'll have really learnt it...

1) Should your handwriting be: a) So fancy with curly bits that it's impossible to read, or b) clear?
2) What size should your capital letters be compared to your small letters? What about 't'?
3) How should you cross out a mistake?
4) Joining words up to make bigger words can make spelling a lot easier. What do you need to do when you put 'full' on the end of a word?
5) What's the rule for when you put 'i' before 'e'? What are the common exceptions?
6) What kind of style should you write in if you were writing as these people: A headmaster, a rap musician, a shop assistant, a professor.
7) What should you always do before you start writing your answer?
8) What are the three steps to get you to essay heaven?
9) What are the three things to work out in your plan for a story?
10) What are the three bits a story needs?
11) When you're writing a story, should the start be *a) dead boring, b) dead exciting* or *c) in Latin* ?
12) What's wrong with these sentences?
    Harold looked at Bert and Bert looked at Harold. He had a green pork-pie hat on.
13) How should you start a formal letter if you don't know the name of the person you're writing to?
    How should you end it? How should you end it if you do know the name of the person you're writing to?
14) Which side should you put your address on? Where should you put the address of the person you're writing to?
15) If you're writing formal language, what could you say instead of these: "won't", "write to or phone", "I got a letter", "can't", "TV"?
16) When you're writing an informal letter, you can use informal language. Do you still have to use sentences?
17) What can you do to stress a point and make your writing more persuasive? What can writing in a personal way be useful for?

Practice/Practise & Advice/Advise

Some words are just plain nasty. They sound the same, but they're not spelt the same.

Practise is a Verb but Practice is a Noun

It's easy to get these two words wrong. Try to remember — when you want a doing word, use practise with an 's'. When you talk about an event or an exercise, use practice with a 'c'.

If it's a thing — it's a noun — use practiCe.

If you can do it — it's a verb — use practiSe.

Roller hockey practice is an exercise. It's a noun so use a 'c'.

I go to hockey practice.

BUT...

I practise my hockey skills.

'practise' is an action you do. Actions are verbs so use an 's'.

It's the same as Advice and Advise

A good way of remembering whether to use practise or practice is to think of advise and advice. Exactly the same rule applies to them — use 's' for a verb, use 'c' for a noun.

Advise and advice are easier to remember because they sound different, while practise and practice sound exactly the same. Don't ask me why.

Coolio advised Victor not to sit down. That's an action. Actions are verbs, so it needs an 's'.

Coolio advised Victor not to sit down.
Victor didn't take Coolio's advice.

Advice is a thing which Victor gets from Coolio. Things are nouns, so you need a 'c'.

'S' for a VERB

I asked Tom to advise me.

I don't want to practise the piano.

'C' for a NOUN

Tom's advice was useless.

I hate piano practice.

Take my advice — practice makes perfect...

The trick to remembering practice/practise is to think of how advice/advise sound. That'll help you remember that you use 's' for the verb and 'c' for the noun.

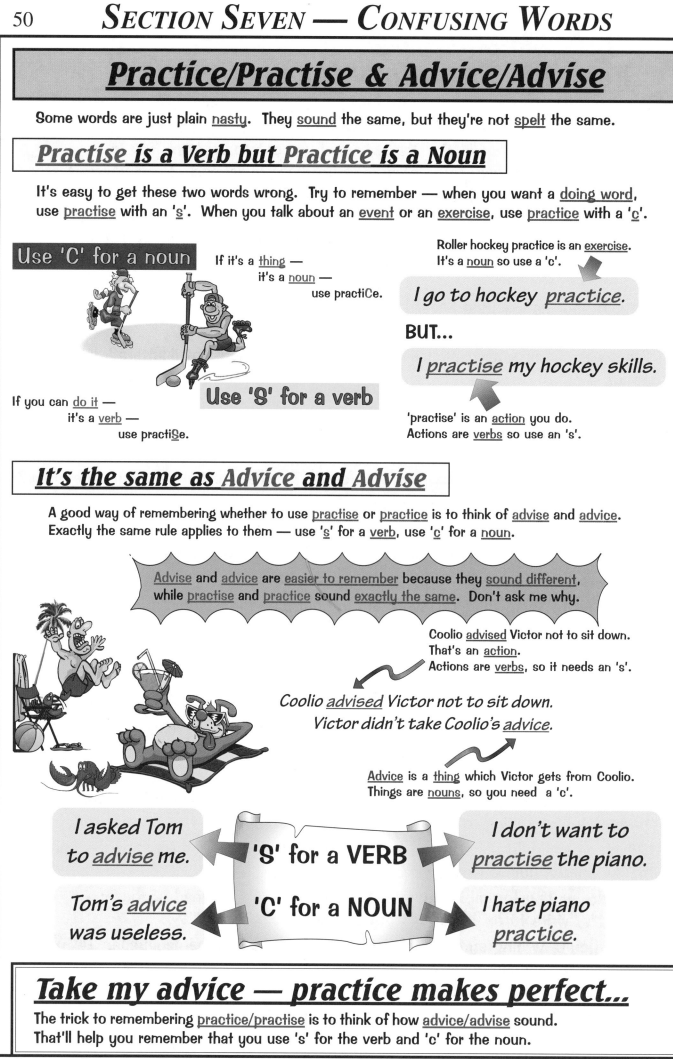

Affect/Effect & Passed/Past

These are more words that sound alike but look different when written and mean different things.

Affect is the Action and Effect is the Result

This one causes loads of mistakes, but it's really dead simple once you know the rule.

Affect is an action. It's a doing word.

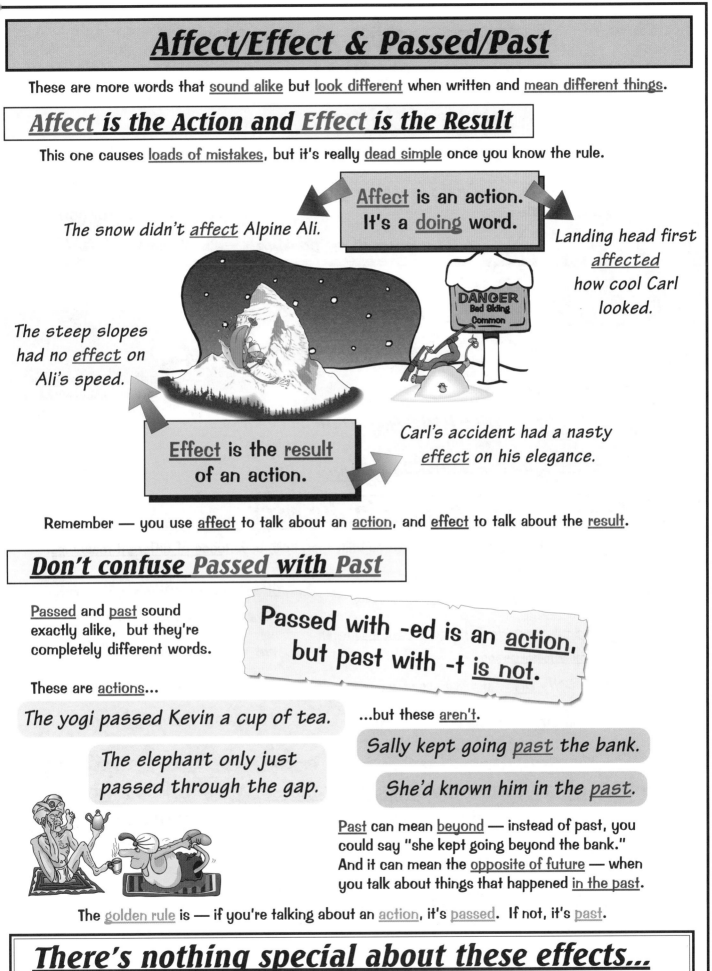

The snow didn't affect Alpine Ali.

Landing head first affected how cool Carl looked.

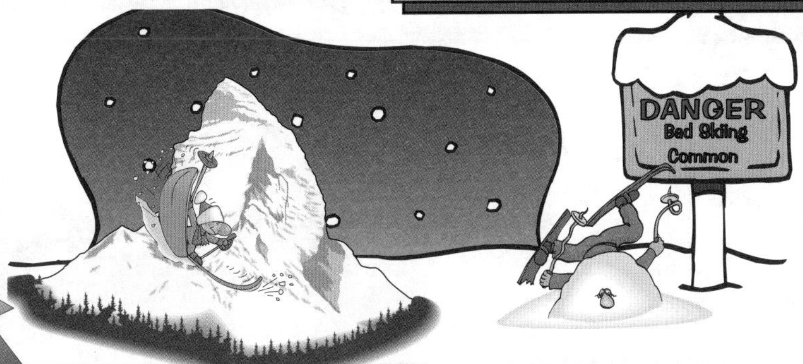

The steep slopes had no effect on Ali's speed.

Effect is the result of an action.

Carl's accident had a nasty effect on his elegance.

Remember — you use affect to talk about an action, and effect to talk about the result.

Don't confuse Passed with Past

Passed and past sound exactly alike, but they're completely different words.

Passed with -ed is an action, but past with -t is not.

These are actions...

The yogi passed Kevin a cup of tea.

The elephant only just passed through the gap.

...but these aren't.

Sally kept going past the bank.

She'd known him in the past.

Past can mean beyond — instead of past, you could say "she kept going beyond the bank." And it can mean the opposite of future — when you talk about things that happened in the past.

The golden rule is — if you're talking about an action, it's passed. If not, it's past.

There's nothing special about these effects...

Try remembering that affect is the action word by thinking that they both start with the letter a. Remember passed is the action word by thinking of the verb pass — verbs are action words.

To/Too/Two and Off/Of

Here are two more annoying sets of words that sound the same but mean different things.

To/Too/Two — they're all Different

You can make mistakes over and over again with these words if you don't know which is which.

① TO means towards or is part of a verb.

Craig is going to bed. = Towards.

His mum likes to sing. = Part of a verb.

② TWO is the number '2'.

Craig weighs two tonnes.

Think of the word 'twice'. Twice means two times. They both start with 'tw'.

③ TOO means "too much" or "also".

This bed's too small... = Too much.

...and it's a bit saggy, too. = Also.

Off/Of — Yet Another Pain in the Neck

It's easy to get of and off confused. Worse still, they both have loads of different meanings.

'Off' often means 'away from'...

Time for take-off. (away from the ground)

I'm off to the shops. (I'm going away from here)

...but it has other meanings too.

Turn the telly off. (the opposite of 'on')

This milk is off. (it's not fresh any more)

'Of' links words together, in lots of ways.

"Beware of the dog."

He went in search of the exit.

He died of his wounds.

He was a friend of mine.

Think of 'of' as a word that links two others. While 'off' is a word on its own that usually means either away from or the opposite of 'on'.

While we're on the subject, never say "off of" — as in "he jumped off of the bridge". It's plain wrong. Say "he jumped off the bridge" or "he jumped from the bridge" instead.

Two more to learn — too important to forget...

There's no easy way out — you have to learn these words until you're sure you know them. If you think you might get confused, stop to check every time you write to, too, two, off or of.

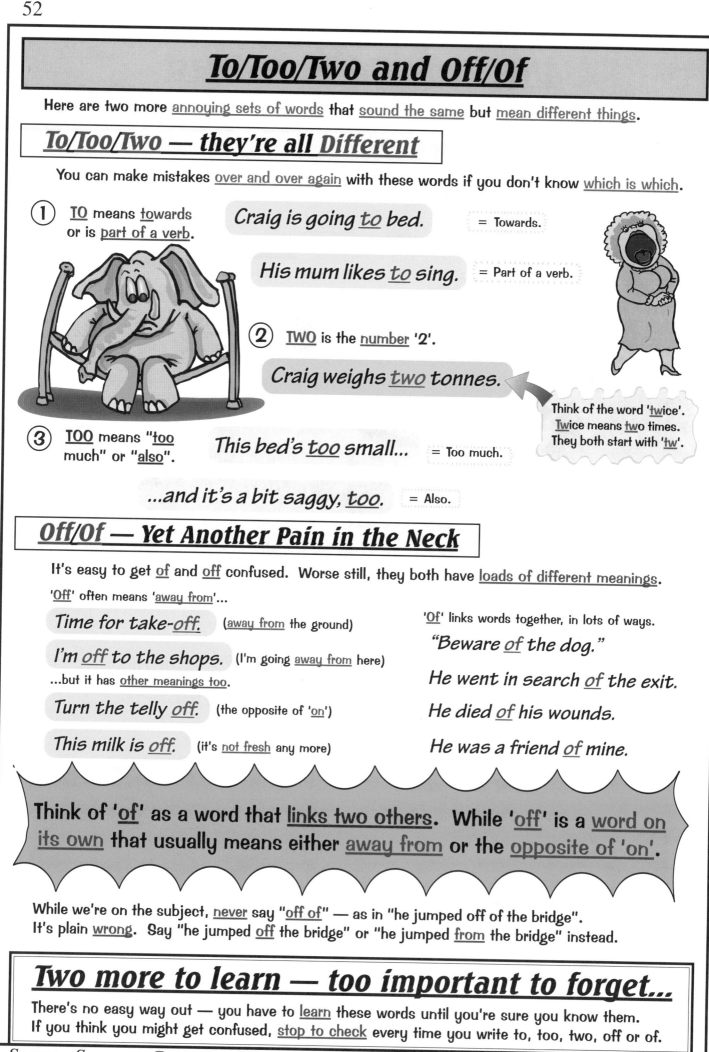

Have/Of, Accept/Except

Loads of people make this mistake — but that doesn't mean it's okay. It isn't. Get it learned.

Should have / Would have / Could have — it's never of

Never use 'of' with could, would, should or might.
Always use 'have' instead.

Sally would have made a good leader.

NOT "Sally would of made a good leader."

I could have been a weightlifter.

NOT "I could of been a weightlifter."

I should have seen it coming.

NOT "I should of seen it coming."

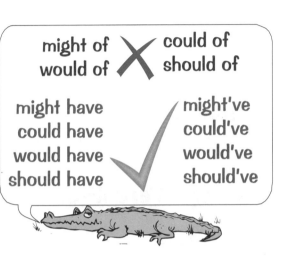

might of
would of
could of
should of

might have
could have
would have
should have

might've
could've
would've
should've

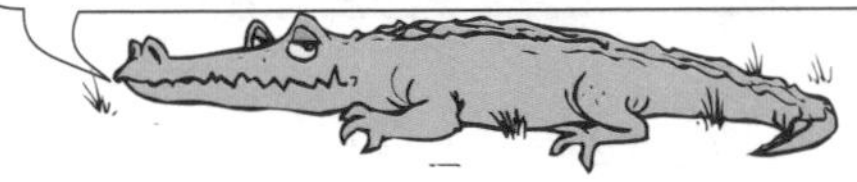

This confuses a lot of people because when you say these sentences, 'have' sounds like 'of'. That's because you often shorten "should have" to "should've" when you speak.

That's okay — it's like saying "I've" instead of "I have", or "you've" instead of "you have". You just have to remember not to be confused by the way "'ve" sounds so much like "of".

Accept is Totally Different from Except

Accept and except sound similar, but don't be fooled — they mean totally different things.
Accept means 'agreeing to' something, or 'receiving' something.
Except means 'not including'.

At first Freda would not accept Bill's Valentine's Day present.

This means she did not want to receive the present.

Bill sweet-talked her until she did accept that a cruise was a cool idea.

This means she did agree to going.

There was nothing there except Freda and Bill.

This means it was only Freda and Bill on the island.

Presents — Exceptionally acceptable...

It may sound like "would of" when you say it, but get clear in your head that it's "would have." Getting confused between accept and except is a silly mistake. Make sure you don't make it.

Hear/Here, Where/Were, There/Their

These three sets of words all sound similar but it looks really bad if you don't know which is which.

Think Twice when You Write 'Here' or 'Hear'

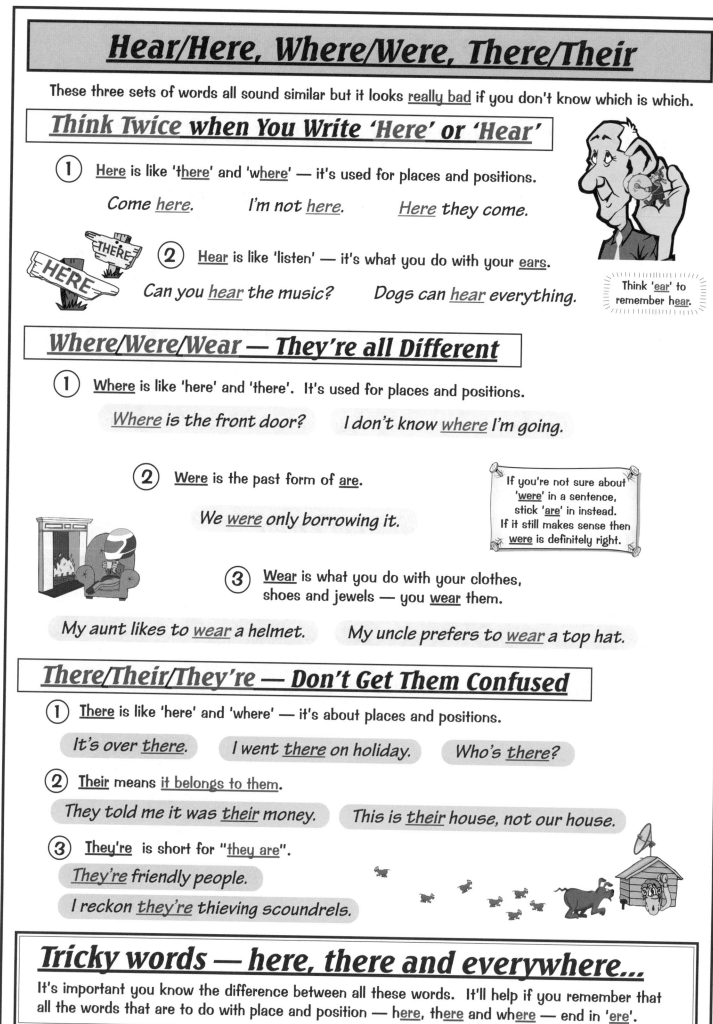

1. Here is like 'there' and 'where' — it's used for places and positions.

   Come here. *I'm not here.* *Here they come.*

2. Hear is like 'listen' — it's what you do with your ears.

   Can you hear the music? *Dogs can hear everything.*

Think 'ear' to remember hear.

Where/Were/Wear — They're all Different

1. Where is like 'here' and 'there'. It's used for places and positions.

   Where is the front door? *I don't know where I'm going.*

2. Were is the past form of are.

   We were only borrowing it.

If you're not sure about 'were' in a sentence, stick 'are' in instead. If it still makes sense then were is definitely right.

3. Wear is what you do with your clothes, shoes and jewels — you wear them.

My aunt likes to wear a helmet. *My uncle prefers to wear a top hat.*

There/Their/They're — Don't Get Them Confused

1. There is like 'here' and 'where' — it's about places and positions.

   It's over there. *I went there on holiday.* *Who's there?*

2. Their means it belongs to them.

   They told me it was their money. *This is their house, not our house.*

3. They're is short for "they are".

   They're friendly people.

   I reckon they're thieving scoundrels.

Tricky words — here, there and everywhere...

It's important you know the difference between all these words. It'll help if you remember that all the words that are to do with place and position — here, there and where — end in 'ere'.

Choose/Chose/Choice, Loose/Lose

Sometimes one tiny letter can change the meaning of a word — watch out for these ones.

Don't Confuse 'Choose', 'Chose' and 'Choice'

① Choose is a verb, a "doing" word. Choose is something that you do.

I have to choose which woman to wrestle.

② Chose is the past form of 'choose'.
Chose is something that you did in the past.

I wonder why she chose to dye her hair blue.

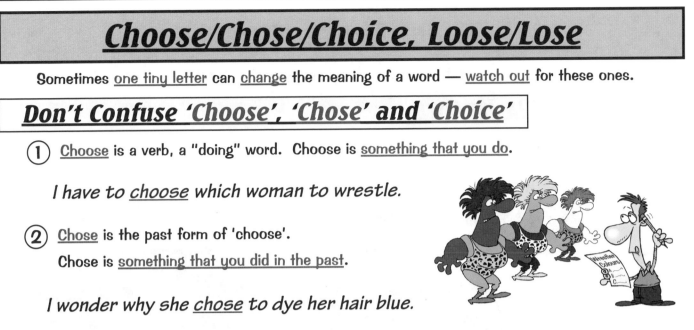

③ Choice is a noun, not a "doing" word. When you choose something, you make a choice.

Hmm — it's a very difficult choice — they all look stronger than me.

Watch Out for 'Loose' and 'Lose' too

It's easy to write 'loose' when you mean 'lose' but they mean completely different things.

Remember, 'loose' does not rhyme with 'choose'. It's 'lose' that rhymes with 'choose'.
'Loose' sounds completely different — like 'moose'. Yeah, it's confusing to me, too.

① Lose is a verb, a "doing" word. It means the opposite of win, or the opposite of find.

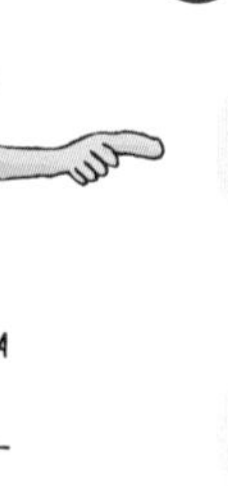

Hurry up or we'll lose the race!

NOT "Hurry up or we'll loose the race."

Keep still or I'll lose my footing.

NOT "Keep still or I'll loose my footing."

② Loose is not a doing word — it's a describing word. It means 'not tight'.

Oh, no! My shorts are loose — they could fall down at any moment.

It's the same with loser. Don't make the mistake of writing 'looser' — that means 'more loose'.

My shorts are even looser than yours. *That means you're a loser.*

The moose is loose — where did you lose it?...

Choose, chose and choice are fiddly little words that you just have to learn to get right.
And you must remember that even though 'lose' sounds similar to 'choose', it has one less 'o'.

Them/Those, Us/Me

'Them' is a word people say a lot — but it's often used wrongly. You have to know what it means.

Them goes On Its Own

'Them' is used instead of a plural name, person, place or thing — it saves you having to repeat the name again. Never ever write 'them' and the name together. That's just wrong.

I went to school with the leopards.

I went to school with them.

NOT "I went to school with them leopards."

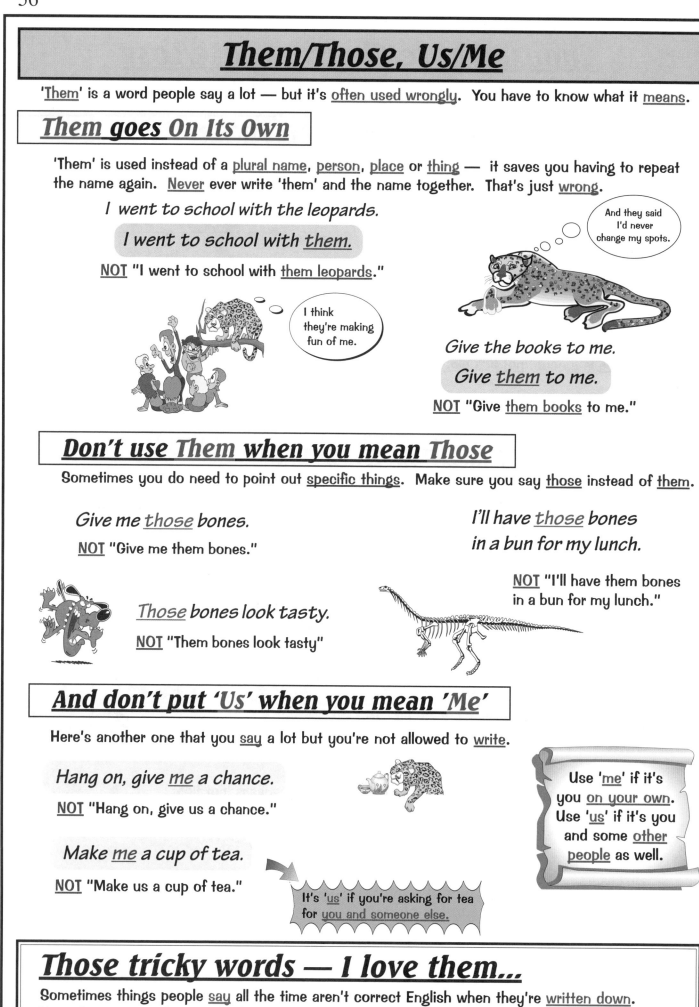

And they said I'd never change my spots.

I think they're making fun of me.

Give the books to me.

Give them to me.

NOT "Give them books to me."

Don't use Them when you mean Those

Sometimes you do need to point out specific things. Make sure you say those instead of them.

Give me those bones.

NOT "Give me them bones."

I'll have those bones in a bun for my lunch.

NOT "I'll have them bones in a bun for my lunch."

Those bones look tasty.

NOT "Them bones look tasty"

And don't put 'Us' when you mean 'Me'

Here's another one that you say a lot but you're not allowed to write.

Hang on, give me a chance.

NOT "Hang on, give us a chance."

Use 'me' if it's you on your own. Use 'us' if it's you and some other people as well.

Make me a cup of tea.

NOT "Make us a cup of tea."

It's 'us' if you're asking for tea for you and someone else.

Those tricky words — I love them...

Sometimes things people say all the time aren't correct English when they're written down. Yes, it's annoying, but you do have to learn how to write them properly.

More Words That Sound Alike

Some of these might look pretty obvious, but some people get them wrong. Make sure you don't.

Would is like Could — Wood is what you get from Trees

Don't fall for this one — if it isn't to do with trees, it's spelt would.

I would if I could.

NOT "I wood if I could."

What would you do without me?

NOT "What wood you do without me?"

When you mean Feel, don't write Fill instead

This mistake makes no sense when you stop and think about it.

Deadlines made her feel annoyed.

NOT "Deadlines made her fill annoyed."

I feel sick.

NOT "I fill sick."

Weather is rain or shine — Whether means If

They're completely different words — you just have to remember which is spelt which way.

What do you mean, perfect weather for ducks?

I love the weather in Britain.

NOT "I love the whether in Britain."

I don't care whether it's hot or cold.

NOT "I don't care weather it's hot or cold."

A Piece is a Little Bit — Peace is when it's Quiet

Yes, I know it's a pain, but you have to get the right vowels in these words.

I need some peace and quiet.

NOT "I need some piece and quiet."

Have a piece of cake.

NOT "Have a peace of cake."

How much wood would a woodchuck chuck?...

Phew, there's a lot of stuff to get your head around on this page. But it's all worth learning. It looks very bad to write a word that sounds like the one you need but has a different meaning.

Did/Done, Saw/Seen

You have to remember when to use did and done. It looks sloppy if you get them mixed up.

Done goes with Have, Has or Had; Did goes On Its Own

A lot of people make the mistake of writing "I done this" or "I done that". It's wrong. There are two ways of saying you did something in the past — "I did" or "I have done".

I did my homework. OR *I have done my homework.*

NOT "I done my homework."

We did what we were told.

OR *We have done what we were told.*

NOT "We done what we were told."

DONE always goes with has, have or had.

DID always goes on its own.

More examples:

Shirley has done her best.
Jake did the crime.
Matt had done his shopping.

Sometimes you can write has, have or had with an extra word before the done — but you still have to use both parts in the sentence.

I have recently done a good thing.
He has always done his best.
What on earth have you done?

It's the same confusion with Saw and Seen

It's exactly the same problem here. Saw is just like 'did' — it needs to be used on its own. Seen is just like 'done' — it has to be used with has, have or had.

I saw an alien. OR *I have seen an alien.*

"I seen an alien."

Jean has not seen the giant fly yet.
The rest of us saw it yesterday.
Have you seen the giant fly?
Were you impressed when you saw it?

SEEN always goes with has, have or had.
SAW always goes on its own.

I've done it all, I've seen it all — now what?...

Yeah, I know it seems a bit picky, but those are the rules and I'm afraid you've got to learn them. It's a common mistake to say "I done" or "I seen" — but it's wrong, so don't write it.

Been/Being, Don't/Doesn't

Don't get 'Been' mixed up with 'Being'

1. You can't use 'been' on its own. You need 'have', 'has' or 'had' with it.

We have been chasing him.
NOT "We been chasing him."

She has been chasing him too.
NOT "She been chasing him too."

2. Sometimes you can have 'being' on its own — don't use 'been' instead.

Stop being scared.
NOT "Stop been scared."

You should try being braver.
NOT "You should try been braver."

3. Usually 'being' is used with 'am', 'is', 'are', 'was' or 'were'.

Been is about what happened in the past. Being is about what's going on now.

Why are you being nasty?
NOT "Why are you been nasty?"

I am being careful.
NOT "I am been careful."

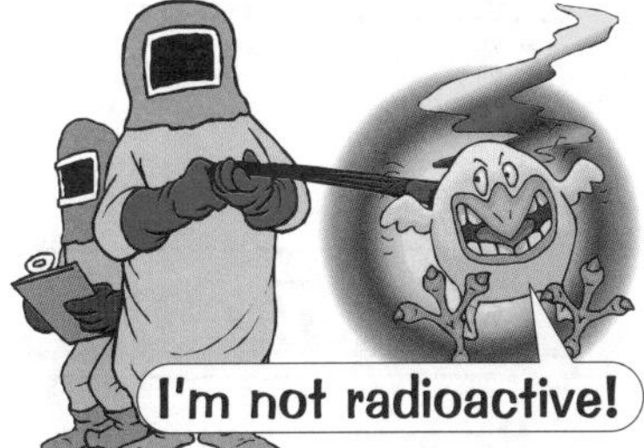
I'm not radioactive!

Don't goes with I, You, We, They; Doesn't with He, She, It

People often say things like 'He don't care'...
Well, the bad news is they're wrong.
There's a big muddle over 'don't' and 'doesn't'.

'Don't' is short for 'do not'.
'Doesn't' is short for 'does not'.

GRRRR!!

My television doesn't work.
NOT "My television don't work."

It doesn't get Channel Five.
NOT "It don't get Channel Five."

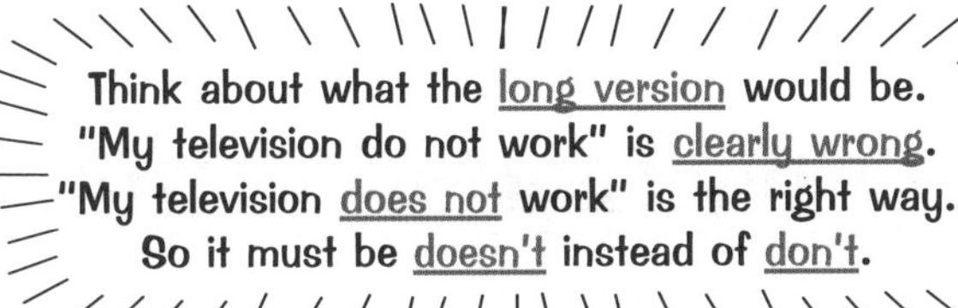

Think about what the long version would be.
"My television do not work" is clearly wrong.
"My television does not work" is the right way.
So it must be doesn't instead of don't.

These are when it's right to use don't:

I don't like red cabbage.
We don't come here often.
You don't want to know.
They don't care about me.

It would be wrong to use don't in these:

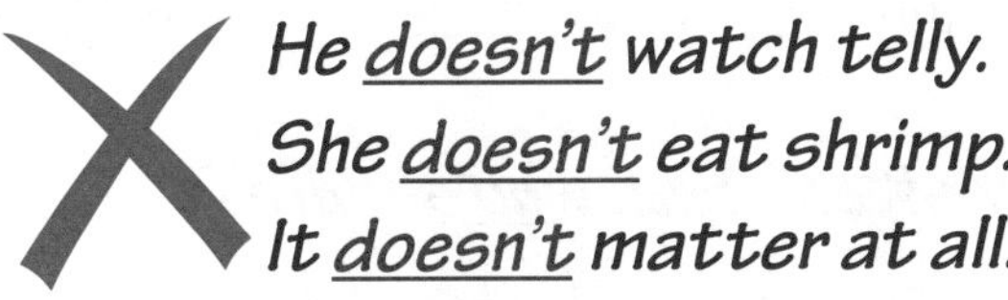

He doesn't watch telly.
She doesn't eat shrimp.
It doesn't matter at all.

Being served? I'll have a doesn't urnips please...

Don't and doesn't are words you use all the time. So it'll be harder to learn the right way if you've been using them wrongly. But you still have to get it right — for he, she or it, you use doesn't.

It's/Its, Who's/Whose

I reckon it's and its cause more problems than anything else in English.
But it's really easy to get them right when you know how. Just learn this rule.

You must use an apostrophe if you mean it is or it has.
If you don't mean it is or it has, don't use an apostrophe.

It's is short for 'it is' or 'it has'

The apostrophe in it's shows that a letter has been left out.
It's with an apostrophe is always short for it is or it has.

Always ask — would this sentence make sense if I wrote 'it is' or 'it has'? If the answer's yes, use it's, not its.

It's raining cats and dogs.

YES — this means "it is raining".

It's been like this for days.

YES — this means "it has been".

Its is Like His or Hers — It Has No Apostrophe

His means something belongs to him, and hers means something belongs to her.
It's exactly the same idea with its — you use its to mean something belongs to it.

You don't use an apostrophe with his or hers so don't use one with its.

Have you fed the beast its dinner?

Remember the question — would it make sense with 'it is' or 'it has'?
NO — "have you fed the beast it is dinner" makes no sense.
And "have you fed the beast it has dinner" is gibberish too.
That means it can't be it's, so it must be its.

It's the Same Idea with Who's and Whose

Think about it — do you mean 'who is' or 'who has'?
If you do, write who's.
If you don't, write whose.

Who's is short for who is or who has.
Whose is about belonging to someone.

I visited Fred, who's a great cook.

YES — this is short for "who is".

I visited Fred, whose food is tasty.

YES — this means the food is Fred's.

Apostrophe — what an apos winner gets...

Loads of people get this wrong but it's really very simple. Could you use it is or it has instead? If you could, put it's. If not, you must put its. It really is as simple as that.

Buy/By/Bye, Know, Through...

One little letter can make a lot of difference. These are mistakes you have to watch out for.

'Buy', 'By' and 'Bye'

1. 'Buy' with a 'u' means getting something in exchange for money.

You can't buy love. *I'm going to buy chocolate.*

The secret here is to learn when to use 'buy' and 'bye'. The rest of the time use 'by'.

2. 'By' is a word that joins two others. It has loads of meanings.

That song is by Steps. *I want it by tomorrow.* *I'll walk by the river.*

3. 'Bye' is short for 'goodbye'.

"Bye, lads!"

Oi!

Don't write 'Now' when you mean 'Know'

'Know' has a 'k' you don't say, just like 'knee' and 'knickers'.

I don't know how they can drink that.

NOT "I don't now how they can drink that."

I know I couldn't.

NOT "I now I couldn't."

Mind the R's in Though, Through, and Thorough

1. Though means 'although', or 'however', or 'despite the fact that...'. It's the easiest one to get right because it has no 'r' in it.

He doesn't weigh much though he's very tall.

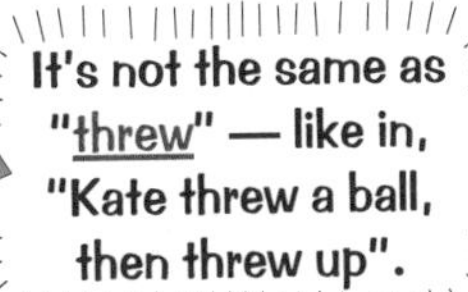
It's not the same as "threw" — like in, "Kate threw a ball, then threw up".

2. Be careful not to miss out the 'r' in through.

The train went straight through her legs.

NOT "The train went straight though her legs."

3. Thorough means complete. Don't forget the extra 'o'.

I gave it a thorough shake.

NOT "I gave it a through shake."

The fat thrush flew through the thorny thicket...

These words are a pain in the neck. They're different, but spelt in annoyingly similar ways. Watch out for them and take care writing them — if you're rushing it's easy to make a mistake.

Teach/Learn, Lend/Borrow, Try To

Lots of people say lend when they mean borrow, and learn when they mean teach. Tut tut...

Lend Something TO Someone, Borrow It FROM Them

Lend means giving something out. Borrowing means taking something from someone. They are exact opposites. If I lend something to you, that means you borrow it from me.

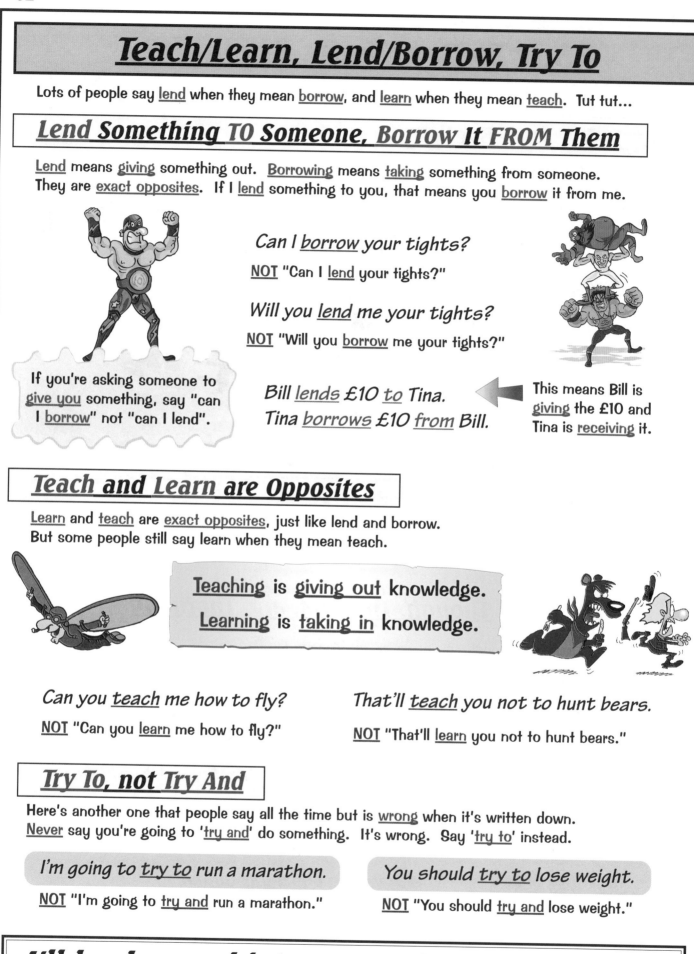

Can I borrow your tights?

NOT "Can I lend your tights?"

Will you lend me your tights?

NOT "Will you borrow me your tights?"

If you're asking someone to give you something, say "can I borrow" not "can I lend".

Bill lends £10 to Tina.
Tina borrows £10 from Bill.

This means Bill is giving the £10 and Tina is receiving it.

Teach and Learn are Opposites

Learn and teach are exact opposites, just like lend and borrow. But some people still say learn when they mean teach.

Teaching is giving out knowledge.
Learning is taking in knowledge.

Can you teach me how to fly?

NOT "Can you learn me how to fly?"

That'll teach you not to hunt bears.

NOT "That'll learn you not to hunt bears."

Try To, not Try And

Here's another one that people say all the time but is wrong when it's written down. Never say you're going to 'try and' do something. It's wrong. Say 'try to' instead.

I'm going to try to run a marathon.

NOT "I'm going to try and run a marathon."

You should try to lose weight.

NOT "You should try and lose weight."

I'll lend you a hint — try to learn this...

You might hear people using lend and borrow or learn and teach as if they mean the same thing. But remember — they're opposites, and you have to get them right when you're writing.

'-one', '-thing', '-body', '-where'

These rules look like they're a bit confusing. They're not really. There's just one rule to learn. All these words that end in 'one', 'body', 'thing' or 'where' are one word apart from 'no one'.

No One is Two Words, Nobody is One Word

These are the two that everyone gets confused.

No one jumped higher.

NOT "Noone jumped higher."

Nobody jumped higher.

NOT "No body jumped higher."

Everyone, Someone, and Anyone are One Word

"Anyone for hurdles?" asked Giant Geoff.

Everyone hated the way Geoff always won.

Someone thought they could beat him.

These are always single words if you're talking about people. The only one that isn't is 'no one'.

Words ending '-thing', '-body' or '-where' are One Word

Everything, anything, something, nothing.

Everybody, anybody, somebody, nobody.

Everywhere, anywhere, somewhere, nowhere.

All these words are one word. Don't be tempted to split them into two.

It chased them everywhere they ran.

Nothing could stop it.

Why wouldn't anybody help them?

An empty grave — there's no body there...

It's simple — all but one of the words that start 'every', 'any', 'some' or 'no' and end 'one', 'thing', 'body' or 'where' are one word. The only tricky one you have to write as two words is 'no one'.

Two Words or One

Watch out for these — they mean different things written as one word or as two words.

Don't write 'across' as 'a cross' or 'apart' as 'a part'

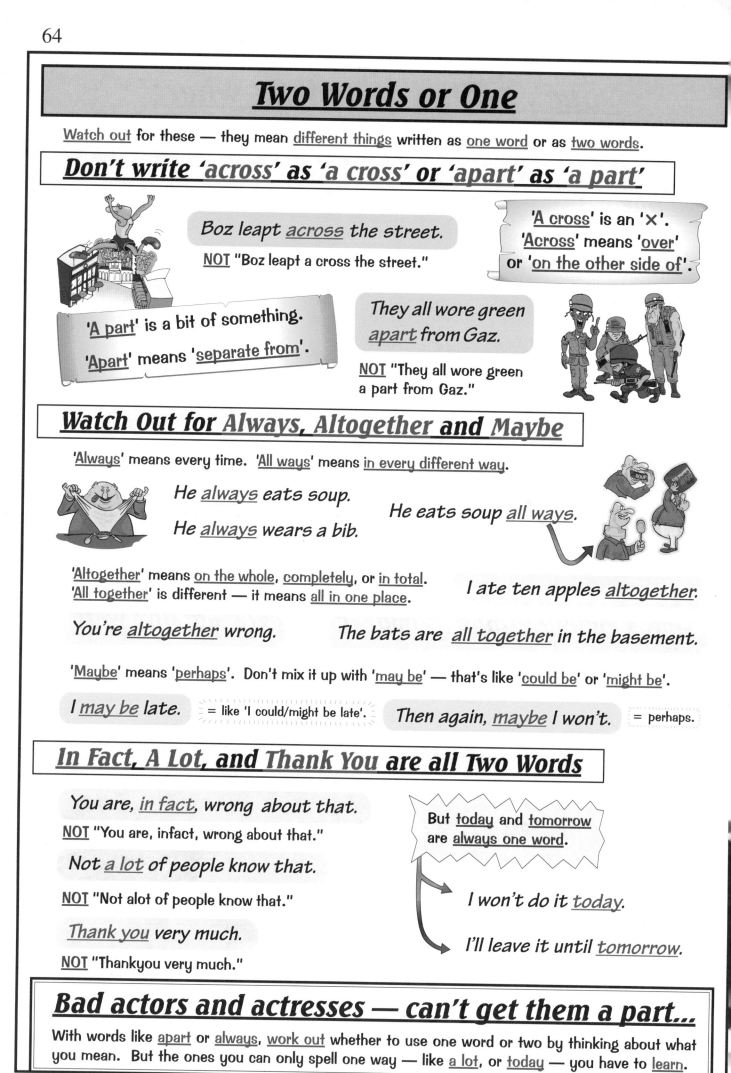

Boz leapt across the street.

NOT "Boz leapt a cross the street."

'A cross' is an 'x'.
'Across' means 'over' or 'on the other side of'.

'A part' is a bit of something.
'Apart' means 'separate from'.

They all wore green apart from Gaz.

NOT "They all wore green a part from Gaz."

Watch Out for Always, Altogether and Maybe

'Always' means every time. 'All ways' means in every different way.

He always eats soup.

He always wears a bib.

He eats soup all ways.

'Altogether' means on the whole, completely, or in total.
'All together' is different — it means all in one place.

I ate ten apples altogether.

You're altogether wrong.

The bats are all together in the basement.

'Maybe' means 'perhaps'. Don't mix it up with 'may be' — that's like 'could be' or 'might be'.

I may be late. = like 'I could/might be late'.

Then again, maybe I won't. = perhaps.

In Fact, A Lot, and Thank You are all Two Words

You are, in fact, wrong about that.

NOT "You are, infact, wrong about that."

Not a lot of people know that.

NOT "Not alot of people know that."

Thank you very much.

NOT "Thankyou very much."

But today and tomorrow are always one word.

I won't do it today.

I'll leave it until tomorrow.

Bad actors and actresses — can't get them a part...

With words like apart or always, work out whether to use one word or two by thinking about what you mean. But the ones you can only spell one way — like a lot, or today — you have to learn.

Always Read the Question

Sounds pretty obvious, doesn't it? But it's easy to forget about it and steam straight in there.

Read the Bit of Writing and the Question Carefully

It doesn't matter if you're doing a comprehension exercise for homework or coursework, or a reading question in an exam — they're all questions that test how well you've understood something you've read. Always do these questions the same way.

Always read carefully through the bit of writing before you start to answer the questions.

Once you've read the bit of writing, you can look at the questions. Do this very carefully too.

Work out what the Question is Asking

All the questions will be about the stuff you've just read. You must read very carefully through each question before you even think about answering it. Always remember the magic question:

What is it asking me to do?

What impression do you get of Mr Smith's attitude to parsnips?

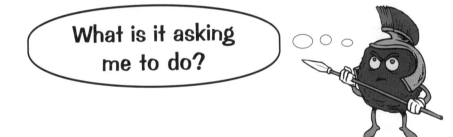

This is asking you to write about what a character thinks and does.

How does the writer make you share Mr Smith's fear of root vegetables?

This is asking you to talk about the writer's choice of words.

Whatever else you do, make sure your answer matches what the question asks you to do. It's amazing how easy it is to slip up this way.

There's no point spending all your time in the first question talking about the writer's choice of words. Even if you do it brilliantly you won't get marks for it.

Questions — always looking for answers...

All this sounds so obvious that it's hardly worth saying, but it's shocking how easy it is to mess up an answer because you haven't thought about exactly what the question is asking you to do.

Answer in Your Own Words...

Okay, there are three things you have to make sure you do when you answer reading questions.

1. Write things down in your own words.
2. Give reasons for what you've said.
3. Back up your reasons with quotes.

It's really important that you remember to do a bit of all of these in your answer. You'll lose out if you only do one or two of them.

Use Different Words from those in the Text

Most of the time, answering "in your own words" just means saying the same thing as the bit of writing says, but in a different way. Sounds like a bit of a cheat, but it's true.

You see, what your teacher wants to know is that you've understood what you've read. If you simply repeat the bit of writing word for word, that doesn't prove anything.

The way to prove you've understood something is to say it again using different words.

Here's a question: Q4 What impression do you get of Mr Smith's attitude to parsnips?

And here's part of the story: "Mr Smith shrank back in fear as I waved the parsnip in front of him."

This answer's not very good — it just says the same thing as the text says.

He shrank back in fear when a parsnip was waved at him.

He is obviously very scared of parsnips.

This answer's better — it shows you understand because it uses new words.

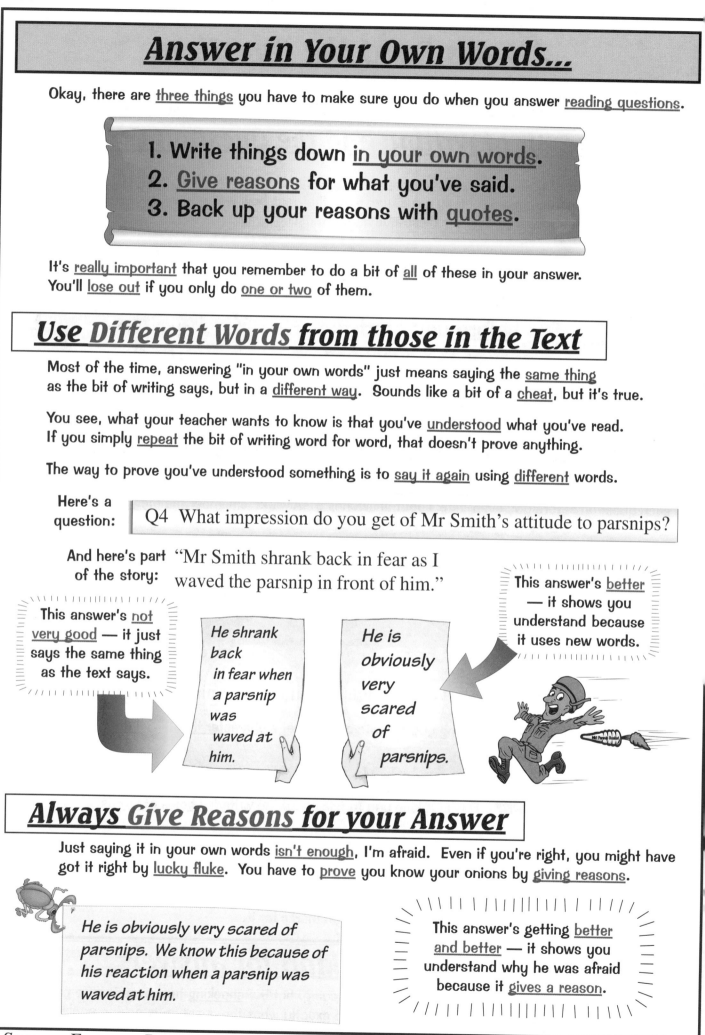

Always Give Reasons for your Answer

Just saying it in your own words isn't enough, I'm afraid. Even if you're right, you might have got it right by lucky fluke. You have to prove you know your onions by giving reasons.

He is obviously very scared of parsnips. We know this because of his reaction when a parsnip was waved at him.

This answer's getting better and better — it shows you understand why he was afraid because it gives a reason.

...And Quote from the Text

Finally, Back Up your Reasons with a Quote

You might think you've done enough by now — you've thought up some words of your own to explain what's going on in the text, and you've given reasons to show that you understand.

Don't throw your brain away yet, there's one more thing you have to do — quote a bit of the text.

He is obviously very scared of parsnips. We know this because of his reaction when a parsnip was waved at him — he "shrank back in fear".

This is now a very good answer — it uses new words, gives a reason, and backs up that reason with a quote.

Teachers love quotes. They show that you've read the text carefully before you answered. Remember — stick loads of quotes in your answer. It'll really help you.

Always put Quotes in Speech Marks

It's vital that you remember to do this. If you don't put speech marks at the start and end of a quote, your teacher won't know that you're quoting, so you won't get credit for it.

Mr Smith shrank back in fear as I waved the parsnip in front of him.

We know this because of his reaction when a parsnip was waved at him — he "shrank back in fear".

These are the words that are in the text, so they need speech marks at the start and end.

There's no need to quote great long chunks of the text. Just a few words will do.

Do all this as Many Times as Possible

That would only be the start of a good answer about Mr Smith and his feelings about parsnips. There'd be tons of other things in the text that you could talk about. The more things you find to talk about, the better you'll do.

The trick is to read through a text and see how many different things you can think of to say. Then use this three-point plan on all of them.

1. Use your own words.
2. Give reasons.
3. Stick in a quote.

Make up a language — use your own words...

Learn the three-point plan for answering reading questions — answer in your own words, give reasons for your answer, and back up your reasons with a quote, in speech marks, from the text.

Giving Opinions

Lots of reading questions want you to prove that you've understood the stuff you've just read. But often you'll get a question that asks for your opinion. You have to say what you think.

Loads of Questions ask you What You Think

Do you think the ending to this story is effective?

Do you think this article will persuade people to eat raw broccoli sandwiches?

Okay, here's the bad news — you need to think a bit more to answer these questions. But don't panic — here's the good news. You can use exactly the same plan to answer them.

1. Say what you think.
2. Give reasons for what you think.
3. Back up your reasons with a quote.

There's No Right Answer to Opinion Questions

The great thing about opinions is you're allowed to disagree with people — even your teacher. Your opinion isn't going to be marked on whether your teacher agrees with it.

What you'll be marked on is whether you make a good argument to support your opinion. That means giving good reasons, and backing them up with quotes.

You have to Give Reasons for What You Think

This is the most important thing to remember. It's not enough just to state an opinion. You have to give reasons why you think that way.

Do you think the ending to this story is effective?

An awful answer — just an opinion, with no reasons.

Yes, I think it's quite effective.

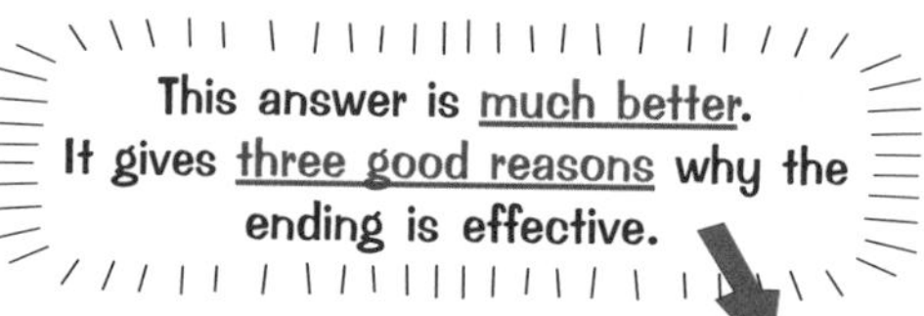

This answer is much better.
It gives three good reasons why the ending is effective.

I think it's an effective ending because it tells us what happens to all the characters. It manages to take us by surprise without being unbelievable. Also it brings the story full circle by answering the question that Jamie asked in the first paragraph.

Don't worry if you can't immediately think of any reasons why. That's quite common. Often you just get a gut reaction about whether you like something.

But you do still need to come up with some reasons. So read the text again, and ask yourself — "What is it about this that makes me like it (or hate it)?"

Giving Opinions

Once you've decided on your reasons, make sure you stick in some quotes from the text.

Use Quotes that are Relevant to your Reasons

It's important that you include loads and loads of quotes from the text.
But don't just quote any old thing — it has to be relevant to the point you're making.

Quoting is well worth doing even if it does feel like a hassle. It'll get you lots of marks.

Try to explain what the quote means as well. That's much better than just quoting.

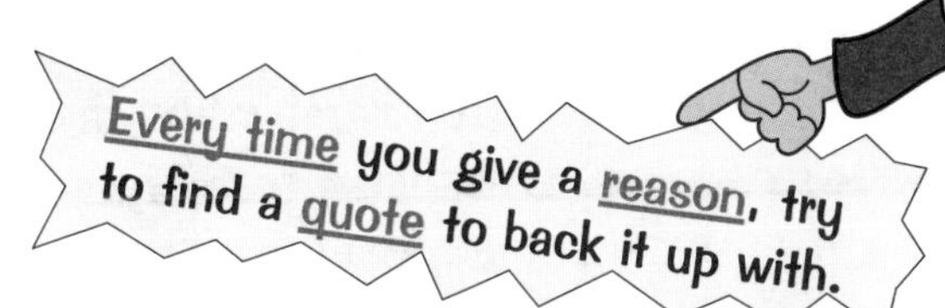

Every time you give a reason, try to find a quote to back it up with.

Do you think this article will persuade people to eat raw broccoli sandwiches?

Eat Your Greens
by Selma Heisenberg

I bet you hate the taste of broccoli. I used to hate it too. But in a recent survey of people who enjoy raw broccoli sandwiches, 67% said they didn't like the taste at first.

Professor Veg Tastic of Oregano State University asked 10,000 people to eat raw broccoli sandwiches and discovered 96% said they felt better for it. The Professor has discovered that a chemical reaction between broccoli and bread releases happy hormones into the brain.

I used to be sceptical but I'm so glad I tried eating raw broccoli sandwiches because now I feel great!

I think it will persuade people to eat raw broccoli sandwiches because the writer uses scientific research to try to convince us. The research sounds impressive because there were a lot of people involved — "10,000 people" — and the results were so overwhelming — "96% said they felt better".

Use quotes to show where your answer comes from. It proves you're not guessing — that way you'll get more marks.

The writer gives an explanation for why people feel better — "a chemical reaction between broccoli and bread releases happy hormones into the brain". That helps to persuade us.

She writes about her own experience by saying "I used to be sceptical", but "now I feel great" after trying the sandwiches. It shows that she was persuaded to like broccoli sandwiches herself, so we ought to be persuaded, too.

This explains why those two quotes are there. It helps the teacher or examiner understand the point you're making.

Double glazing exam — give a good quote...

Don't just say "I like it" or "I think it's boring". You have to say why. That's often something you have to think about a lot. Always give reasons, and always back them up with quotes.

Reading Test — Text

Read through this article. Then look at the example questions and answers on the next three pages.

Plans to build an 80 metre high sculpture of a fish have caused controversy in the village of Crosby. The Millennium Fish will cost £750,000 and will be paid for out of funds raised by the weekly tombola at the Crosby Community Centre.

I visited Crosby last week and found that most local residents are furious that the money is not instead being used to buy new equipment for the local hospital or new books for the school library.

Agatha Crumb, who has lived in the village all her life, had a typical comment: "It's disgusting, that's what it is. Nobody wants this stupid fish. I wouldn't have done the tombola every week if I'd known they were going to spend the money on this."

Brian Dribble feels so strongly about it that he has set up a campaign group, Crosby People Against the Fish. Mr Dribble and his colleagues have spent the last month standing outside the local supermarket asking people to sign a petition against the Fish. "I've got over 500 signatures," he says. "Only 1000 people live in Crosby so that means over half of them have signed our petition."

I talked to 20 people when I was in Crosby, and 16 of them said they were opposed to the Fish. Two of the other four liked the idea, and two said they didn't have an opinion.

But Councillor Charlie Elk, leader of Crosby District Council, said he was going to press ahead with plans for the Fish despite local opposition. "I think it will really put Crosby on the map," he said. "It will bring in a lot of tourists, and that can only be good for businesses in the town."

The idea for the Fish has come from the world-famous sculptor Darius Fridge, winner of several sculpture competitions. Mr Fridge was also responsible for the Millennium Duckling, a giant sculpture of a duckling built in Thornton two years ago.

Darius Fridge says he understands the concerns of the local people. "It happens all the time," he says. "The people of Thornton hated the idea of the giant duckling, but now that it's there they really like it. They feel it gives their town an identity."

As for me, I understand why the local people would rather have the money spent on schools and hospitals, but I think the idea of a giant fish sculpture is a worthwhile one — life would be very dull and boring if we didn't have big works of art to brighten it up.

I'm sure that the people of Crosby will grow to love the Fish and in a few years will wonder how they ever managed without it.

Millennium Fish
Exclusive
Fear for sanity in Crosby

Reading Test — Questions

Now it's time to have a look at some questions on what you've just read. These are the kind of questions you'll get asked in reading tests.

Find the Facts in the Article

1. Write down two things the article tells us about the sculptor Darius Fridge.

The article says several things about Darius Fridge, but the question only asks for two of them. You could put any two of these.

He came up with the idea for the Fish.
He is world-famous.
He has won several sculpture competitions.
He built the Millennium Duckling.
He understands the concerns of Crosby people.

You need to Think to Find Reasons

2. What arguments are given in favour of the Millennium Fish being built?

'Arguments' here just means reasons.

This is a bit more difficult. You have to look through the article and find as many arguments as you can in favour of the Fish being built.

There aren't any arguments in favour of the Fish at all in the first five paragraphs. Whatever you do, don't panic and start writing things down that aren't relevant.

It will put the town on the map.

There are two arguments in the sixth paragraph, both given by Charlie Elk.

It will bring in tourists, and that will be good for business.

These mean it will make the town more famous.

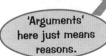

This one's a bit less obvious. It isn't something that the article tells you directly — you have to work it out for yourself.

3 *Even though local people don't like the idea now, they might like it later. The writer says he thinks they will "grow to love it". The people of Thornton didn't like their sculpture at first, but they like it now.*

Life would be very dull and boring if we didn't have big works of art to brighten it up.

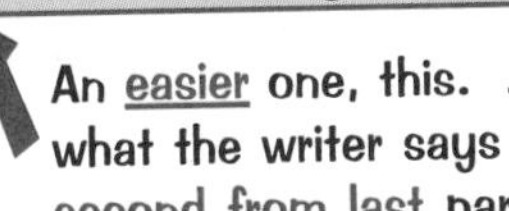

An easier one, this. Just copy what the writer says in the second from last paragraph.

Millennium Fish — you want chips with that?
Official Sponsor Crosby Millennium Fish

Name these rushes — that's a reed-ing test...

All the answers are there in the text. You won't find them just by glancing at it, though. Read it really carefully. Sometimes you have to think a bit to spot a hidden answer.

Reading Test — Questions

Now here's a question that's a bit more difficult. It asks for the "impression" you get from the article, which means you have to put the answer in your own words.

3. What impression do you get of the local people's attitude towards the Fish?

The Perfect Answer gets Straight to the Point

Most local people don't like the Fish. One woman, Agatha Crumb, says the Fish is "disgusting". We know this is a view lots of local people share because the writer says it is a "typical" comment. Also the woman says "nobody wants this stupid fish". This shows that other people agree with her.

The article tells us that one man "feels so strongly about it that he has set up a campaign group". He says that over half the people who live in Crosby have signed his petition. This shows that most people in Crosby don't want the Fish.

The writer says he talked to 20 local people and "16 of them said they were opposed to the Fish". 16 out of 20 is quite a lot, so this is another reason to think that most local people are against it.

The writer did find two local people who liked the Fish — "two of the other four liked the idea" — and two more who didn't mind. This shows that there are a small number of local people who do like the Fish.

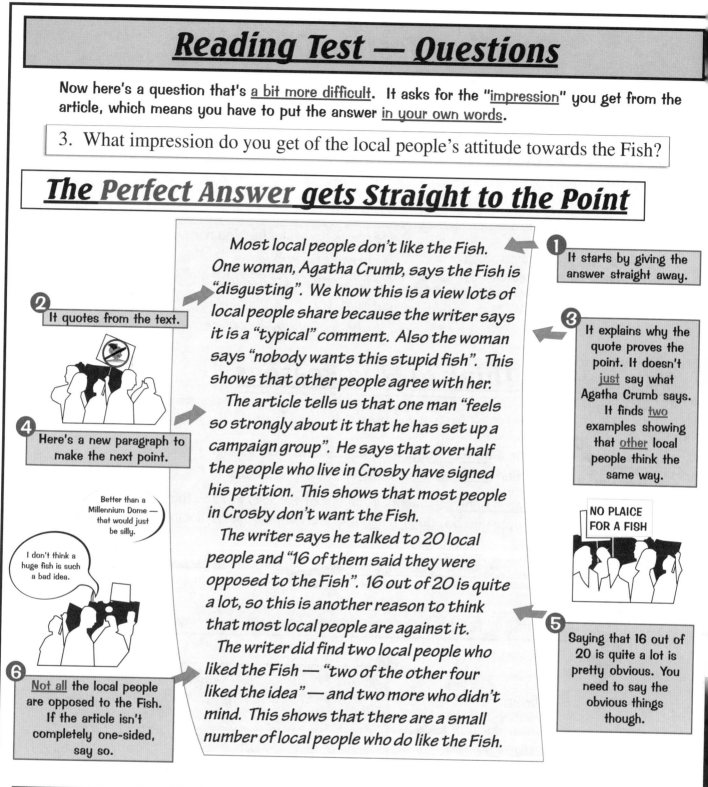

1. It starts by giving the answer straight away.

2. It quotes from the text.

3. It explains why the quote proves the point. It doesn't just say what Agatha Crumb says. It finds two examples showing that other local people think the same way.

4. Here's a new paragraph to make the next point.

Better than a Millennium Dome — that would just be silly.

I don't think a huge fish is such a bad idea.

5. Saying that 16 out of 20 is quite a lot is pretty obvious. You need to say the obvious things though.

6. Not all the local people are opposed to the Fish. If the article isn't completely one-sided, say so.

If it's Not in the Question, Don't put it in the Answer

That "perfect answer" doesn't talk about anything that isn't in the question. The question asks what local people think about the fish. It would be wrong to talk about what Darius Fridge thinks, because he's not a local person. Don't talk about what the writer thinks because he isn't a local person either.

Reading "TEST" — easy, it's only four letters...

These are the questions where you really have to use lots of quotes. For one thing, they prove you've read the article and you aren't just making it all up. Say why you've used a quote, and don't be afraid to state the bleeding obvious. The clearer you make your point, the better.

Reading Test — Questions

Opinion questions are Hard — No Right Answer

4. Do you think the arguments for or against the Fish are more persuasive?

No right or wrong answer? That seems a bit weird. Don't worry, though. It means that it doesn't matter which side you agree with, but how you make your point.

To prove it, I'm going to give you bits from two answers — one that argues each side of the debate. Both would get fantastic marks because they give reasons and quote from the article.

1 You can write a Perfect Answer AGAINST the Fish...

Start by saying what your opinion is, then quote from the article to back it up.

Give your most important point first.

I think the arguments against the Fish are more persuasive. The most important argument is that you could use the money on schools or hospitals — "most local residents are furious that the money is not instead being used to buy new equipment for the local hospital or new books for the school library."

I don't think Charlie Elk's arguments are very good. He says it will "put Crosby on the map" and "be good for businesses". It's obvious that most local people don't like the idea and I think he should listen to what they say. It doesn't seem fair to force them to have the Fish if they don't want it.

This is great. Give an opposing point of view, then say why you don't agree with it.

2 ...or a Perfect Answer FOR the Fish

Again, you say what your opinion is, then quote from the article to back it up.

I think the arguments for the Fish are more persuasive. I agree with the writer that "life would be very dull and boring if we didn't have big works of art to brighten it up." My uncle lives near a big statue of an Angel in Gateshead. I see it when I go to visit him and I think it is very impressive.

This is good — it's okay to talk about your personal experience in questions that ask for your opinion.

The article says local people want the money to be spent on the hospital or the school instead. I agree that hospitals and schools are important but I think art is important too because it's fun and it makes life more interesting.

If you think the arguments you disagree with aren't completely wrong, don't be afraid to say so.

No right answers — no left ones either...

The whole "no right answer" thing seems to make no sense, but it's really about how well you write and whether you quote bits from the text. That's honestly all there is to it.

Revision Summary for Sections 7 & 8

This stuff's quite fun. That's what I reckon, anyway. You get to read about fish and stuff like that. The Confusing Words section is a bit more boring, but you really do need to know it to do well in English. So, it's another page of questions to check you know it all. I know you'd rather watch TV — so would I, but if you learn this you'll do stacks better at English. It's that simple.

1) Which of these are OK?
   I did the washing up. I done the washing up. I have done the washing up.
2) What about these?
   I saw him break all the plates. I seen them smash. I have seen him juggle.
3) Correct these sentences:
   I been to the park everyday this week. I am been healthy.
4) Rewrite this sentence correctly:
   I don't like listening to tapes because my tape player don't sound very good.
5) There's one mistake in each of these sentences. Find the mistakes:
   It's been a long time since the hall had it's last concert. Its a real shame. "Whose on?" you ask. It's the Donkeys, who's recent single "Eat Some Hay" shot to number 97 in the local charts.
6) When should you use 'buy', 'by' and 'bye'?
7) Correct this sentence: "Buy, I'm off to by a book bye Byron."
8) What do though, through and thorough mean?
9) What's the difference between 'lend' and 'borrow'?
   What about 'teach' and 'learn'?
10) Which of these need a space: nothing, nobody, anything, anyone, noone, everyone, someone.
11) What's the difference between 'always' and 'all ways'?
    What about 'altogether' and 'all together'?
12) What should you work out before you start to answer a question?
13) What are the three things you should do when answering reading questions?
14) Why should you always put things in your own words, instead of just copying bits from the text?
15) What should you do to back up your answer?
16) Should you <u>always</u> put quotes in speech marks?
17) When you have an opinion question, what are the three things you should do in your answer?
18) If there's something really obvious that backs up your answer, should you:
    a) not say anything because it's too obvious, or b) point it out because it backs up your point?

Index

Index